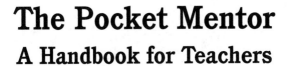

The Pocket Mentor
A Handbook for Teachers

Chris A. Niebrand

Elizabeth L. Horn

Robina F. Holmes

Allyn and Bacon
Boston London Toronto Sydney Tokyo Singapore

to our fathers

Robert R. Auth

George J. Lentzner

Charles E. Holmes

Copyright © 2000 by Allyn & Bacon
A Pearson Education Company
Needham Heights, MA 02494

Internet: www.abacon.com

A previous edition was published by J. Weston Walch
Publisher, copyright © 1992.

Between the time website information is gathered then
published, it is not unusual for some sites to have closed.
Also, the transcription of URLs can result in unintended
typographical errors. The publisher would appreciate
notification where these occur so that they may be corrected
in subsequent editions. Thank you.

Library of Congress Cataloging-in-Publication Data

Niebrand, Chris A.
    The pocket mentor : a handbook for teachers / Chris A. Niebrand,
Elizabeth L. Horn, Robina F. Holmes.
        p.   cm.
    Includes bibliographical references and index.
    ISBN 0-205-29693-9 (alk. paper)
    1. Teachers—United States—Handbooks, manuals, etc.   2. Teaching—
United States—Handbooks, manuals, etc.   3. Classroom management—
United States—Handbooks, manuals, etc.   I. Horn, Elizabeth L.
II. Holmes, Robina F.   III. Title.
LB1775.2.N54   2000
371.102—dc21   98-54370
                                                                    CIP

Printed in the United States of America

10   9   8   7   6   5   4   3   2   03   02

contents

Chapter 3
The Classroom 35

Chapter 4
Curriculum: Design Strategies 63

Chapter 5
Curriculum: Implementation 103

Chapter 6
Record Keeping   152

Chapter 7
Liabilities, Safety, and the Unexpected   164

Chapter 8
Administrators

preface

Research focusing on school—and it is extensive—consistently indicates that a primary factor in determining school quality and student success is the classroom teacher. The quality of any teacher is continually improved through mentoring. We grow from being mentored as well as from mentoring others.

Our goal was to write a book to help others entering the field of education. While attempting to mentor others, we found ourselves surrounded by a willing support system within our profession. We also recognized the essence of our teaching philosophies: that when we help our colleagues by sharing a teaching strategy or curriculum idea, we strengthen our profession and ultimately improve the education of our students.

We hope that you, the reader, will examine the suggestions contained within and apply them as you see fit for the benefit of your teaching and, ultimately, your students.

ACKNOWLEDGMENTS

The Pocket Mentor was not created on the upper floors of a research library or out of hours spent peering at a computer monitor. Nor is it a compilation of the teaching experiences of three teachers in Boise, Idaho. Rather, it is a blend of the stories that make up the careers of all the people who touched our lives. Through these stories and discussions we have tried to filter out the essence of what a person needs to do to be successful in the classroom. We acknowledge all those people who influenced who we are as teachers and how we view teaching.

In the first edition, we listed all the wonderful people who advised and counseled us, helping us form our philosophies into words. For this edition, we must offer a general acknowledgment to all of you who have helped us. Otherwise, we would have had to print a multivolume text listing every mentor, teacher, protégé, student teacher, parent, administrator, and student who has taught us one more vitally important thing about teaching.

As with any production, *The Pocket Mentor* is a result of the efforts of many. We would like to thank those who reviewed the manuscript: Lorraine Gerstl, Santa Catalina School, Carmel, CA; Monica S. Hornburg, Thayer Academy, Braintree, MA; and Eileen Madaus, The Franklin Elementary School, Newton, MA; and thanks to the countless new teachers and mentors we've worked with over the years.

All of you are part and parcel of this book. Thank you.

Chris, Liz, and Robin

introduction

Mentoring: Why This Book

Since our last book, a whirlwind of change has swept through the schoolhouse. Elementary and secondary students are conducting research projects online, the diversity of our student population has required more curricula that is multicultural, and the classroom has become a place where the "gifted" student works cooperatively with the slow learner. Technology has created exciting opportunities and challenges for both students and teachers; in many cases, teachers are running to keep up with their young, technologically savvy charges.

Other, less desirable, obstacles also face today's teachers. Violence is a reality, and security systems that we've come to expect in airports and government buildings are on the increase in our schools. Although most of what we've advocated in our classes, seminars, and writing is still sharply relevant, these rapid changes in our culture have caused us to reassess and revise. What has *not* altered, however, is that the success of any teacher's school year can be traced to that all-important first day.

Like weddings, funerals, and graduation, first days of school are milestones that conjure memories of warm fuzziness or goose-pimply horror. How you deal with this day is critical to your students and you, and, most importantly, how the rest of the year will unfold. You set the tone.

The Faculty

Mike	Mary	Barbara	Bill
Kindergarten	*Secondary Reading*	*Language Arts Junior High*	*Spanish High School*

Marc	Gary	Tami	Nick
Math Junior High	*Humanities High School*	*Science High School*	*Band High School*

Allen	Kathy	Brian	Ellen
Math Junior High	*6th Grade*	*Social Studies High School*	*4th Grade*

Even if you are a veteran teacher, a change in building, curriculum, or room represents starting over. Changes require preparation. Although these alterations in your career may be exciting and challenging, they do bring new problems and frustrations. This is all the more reason to establish an appropriate learning environment from the beginning.

As students and teachers, we have all suffered through awkward beginnings. The three of us have been there. Even though our situations dif-

Robert
2nd/3rd Grade

Betty
Language Arts
High School

Gerry
Vocal Music
High School

Jeff
Science/Coach
High School

Katie
P.E.
Junior High

Sharon
Media Specialist
Middle School

Melanie
History/Coach
Secondary

Angie
School Secretary
Elementary

fered, we remember our initial months in new teaching assignments as frustrating, tearful, and stressful. Fortunately, these periods passed. What saved us was the knowledge that we weren't alone.

The year we (Chris and Liz) met proved to be the toughest we'd encountered before and since. Although there were several reasons for this, we traced much of that grim experience back to the first day of class. It was a nightmare.

Because of similar plights, we became kindred spirits. Both of us had transferred from junior highs and were facing a new environment, new curricula, and a new administration. Chris was replacing a well-liked veteran teacher of an accelerated class. She faced many hostile juniors who were afflicted with a severe case of teacher loyalty—to the old teacher. As a result, Chris's new students entered the class as reluctant learners, doubting the credibility of anyone replacing the previous instructor. Liz faced five classes of "at risk" students. The classes were large, ranging in size from thirty-two to thirty-eight of the most notorious shoplifters and substance abusers in the community. These students were challenge enough, but our classrooms presented even more obstacles in those first weeks of school.

We'd received our schedules for adjoining rooms—which evolved into a blessing—in a remodeled wing of an ancient building. Desks were "on order." Shadeless windows faced a southern exposure. The scarred hardwood floor, freckled with paint, resembled a Jackson Pollock canvas. Carpeting was due to arrive "any day." We were told not to put anything on the walls until the room renovation was complete. Consequently, students had a difficult time establishing a feeling of community and belonging. A few folding chairs and tired, graffitied desks were clumped in the hot little rooms that faced a hectic, downtown street. We were always party to the traffic and screams of the YMCA daycare playground across the street. On Mondays, garbage was collected; Tuesdays were lawn-mowing days. Chris especially remembers reading Dylan Thomas's *Do Not Go Gentle into That Good Night* to the accompaniment of a leaf blower. So much for tone.

A couple of colleagues took pity. With their help, and the detective work of the custodians, we eventually obtained teacher-sized desks. The middle drawer of Chris's was broken and frequently fell out, resulting in a floor confettied with staples, pens, and pencils; she and the students got used to that. We were able to scavenge cinder blocks and boards for shelves; cardboard boxes or plastic milk cartons served as temporary file cabinets. In time, all this equipment trickled in, but the first weeks of class were an experience that we'd equate with frequent trips to the dentist for root canal work.

❧

My (Robin's) case was entirely different. Right after student teaching, I was fortunate enough to simply slide into my supervising teacher's position. Everything was familiar; the climate had

been established, the rules had been presented, and the parents and students had already accepted me. I knew my way around the school. This situation was any beginning teacher's dream come true.

Twelve years later, I transferred to a new school in a larger district. Even though I was a veteran teacher, I found myself in the same frightening predicament as a novice—alone, needing materials and friendly colleagues. My teaching assignment was a combined second/third grade classroom in a school serving an affluent section of the city. Parents were immediately concerned that their third graders would not be challenged enough in the combined class. The second graders' parents worried that their children were being taught material beyond their abilities. I not only had to get used to a new school and class, but also had to demonstrate my competency to the parents.

During the second week of school, a local television crew interviewed me about how a mixed class functions. I did my best to handle the interview as a professional, to educate parents, and to resume teaching. I tried to rely on my previous years of experience.

But, if you are not an experienced teacher, whom do you trust? Where do you find answers? How can you identify what you need to know? Who cares enough to help you?

The story of Odysseus tells of his wife, Penelope, and son, Telemachus, who were left on the island of Ithaca while Odysseus was fated to wander for ten years. Because of his lengthy absence, the people of Ithaca assumed that Odysseus was dead. Rude, greedy men spent days in his great hall, slaughtering livestock, consuming his food and wine, and tormenting his family. Frustrated with the intrusions, Penelope and Telemachus felt helpless. The goddess Athena took pity on Telemachus. In the guise of the great Ithacan Mentor, she visited him and offered comfort and encouragement. Inspired by her guidance, Telemachus found the inner strength to embark on the journey that would find his father and restore the house to peace.

Ideally, a guardian angel figure will appear miraculously at your side—a mentor who will nurture you and tell you how to handle discipline. This mentor will tell you where to find a copy of the curriculum, e-mail access, or the rest room. How nice it would be to know that you should take your gradebook or disk along during fire drills, that you must write progress reports, and that you must keep accurate daily records!

We wish we'd known what to do about cheating, make-up work, or procedures for admitting new students to class. We wished someone had told us what to do when a fight breaks out in the classroom, or a student comes consistently late to class, or when every computer in the lab crashes, simultaneously. We wish that we, like Telemachus, had had a mentor to offer encouragement and advice as we began our teaching odyssey.

After that first nightmarish year, we made a pact to offer new teachers the guidance we'd never had. We've attempted to ease the way for those teachers who need help with curriculum decisions, discipline problems, and the daily routines that govern the business of teaching.

When the idea clicked to write our first book, we had come to the realization that all new teachers, regardless of grade level or assignment, need mentoring. This is not a book of statistics or absolutes; it is an anecdotal handbook based on battle scars acquired during more than fifty years of combined teaching experience from kindergarten to college. It represents years of graduate work, articles written and published, grants, seminars, workshops taken and presented, and trial and error.

As we were writing, we often discussed whether there was a need to separate sections dealing with elementary and secondary strategies. We ultimately found that we had, in most cases, common concerns and common solutions.

This handbook offers advice for all levels and disciplines. We believe that teaching is universal with universal goals. Teaching can be difficult and stressful, yet filled with successes and rewards.

We intend that this book serve as your mentor until you locate that guardian angel in your profession who will answer all your questions before you know enough to ask them. It can assist you in establishing goals and priorities. This book and a healthy sense of humor will launch you on your journey as a beginning teacher. Welcome!

chapter one

Professionalism

My advice for new teachers is simple. Teach from the heart; put your soul into your work rather than just rattling off facts or philosophies. Make it real and lively. We don't just want to hear about history or English; we want to taste it, touch it, smell it, love it. Teach with passion and intensity, and while you're at it, try to be fair and diplomatic.

— Molly Campbell

Teaching is a public profession. Being a teacher means you work and live in the public arena. The people in your community will perceive you as a teacher both in and out of school. For better or worse, this means you have to be aware of the impression you make, in school and in your community. The majority of this book is devoted to the art and science of teaching, but this opening chapter offers you tips on professionalism and living your private life in the public eye.

Experienced teachers may recognize some of these situations and groan, "How well I know." Beginning teachers may gasp, "I never would have thought of that—now at least I'm prepared."

DRESSING FOR THE JOB

One day a student in Marc's junior high math class asked Marc, "Why do you always wear a tie? My English teacher doesn't." The question caught Marc off guard, and his immediate reply was, "Because I'm a professional." Thinking about it later, Marc realized that there was more to it than that. He recognized that dressing up each day added to his self-confidence, established a difference between him and his students, and conveyed a message that said, "I value myself and what I do."

If you are a beginning teacher, you need to understand the reasons for establishing your role as teacher and professional. If you are within ten years of the ages of your students, one of the most challenging tasks ahead of you will be defining your role as the teacher and the one in charge. If you dress, talk, and act like your students, they will see you as a peer, and you will embark on a frustrating journey. Begin to establish yourself as someone students can respect from the first moment you meet.

If you are a beginning teacher, you will probably not possess an extensive professional wardrobe. The important point is that you should look and act like an adult in a professional situation. Numerous books and magazines address this subject.

No one expects a teacher to wear a suit every day. If your day will involve sitting on the floor or using paints and glue, you'll adjust accordingly. If you're being formally evaluated, meeting with parents or colleagues, or having a school holiday program, you'll want to look as professional as possible. Your dress will depend on the climate and mores of your community. If your administration expects ties and jackets for men and hose for women, comply. Even if your school doesn't have this kind of a standard, keep in mind that you are representing a profession and, most importantly, establishing yourself as your students' teacher and model.

In many communities, Fridays are more casual and school shirts are worn. If this applies to your situation, wear school apparel when it's appropriate.

LANGUAGE AND THE CLASSROOM

Professional educators do not use obscene language in the classroom, nor do they permit their students to do so. The use of appropriate language models speech patterns that students can adopt for lifetime use. Profanity debases the educational situation and the people involved. Swearing at a class is condescending to your students and sets a poor example. Even if you are thinking vile thoughts, don't say them. A large part of what we are trying to convey is respect for self and others. Students need to learn that there is a time and a place for appropriate behavior, and school is such a place.

Dealing with Questions

Students, like most people, are curious. They will want to find out things about you. Some will ask personal questions innocently and politely, while others, if permitted, will blurt a question when you least expect it: "Ms. Jones, are you married?" or "Mr. Thomas, how many kids do you have?" Some students have very few positive role models in their lives. You may be their only example, and they are eager to see what makes you tick. Sometimes it is a ploy to divert your attention from the lesson.

If the question is blurted out and it is one you would normally feel comfortable answering, remind the student that interrupting is not appropriate, but that if he or she asks you at the end of class, you'll respond then. If the question is rudely stated or makes you uncomfortable, state simply that you will speak with the student after class, and proceed with the lesson. After class, discuss with the student the inappropriateness of asking personal questions in public settings. You might turn it around and ask how the student would feel being asked a question in front of a group of people.

Sometimes during a discussion, students will ask your opinion on a controversial topic, such as abortion, capital punishment, or a political candidate. Many teachers employ the strategy of Socrates, questioning students in return. If you do choose to share your opinion, be sure to state that it is simply your opinion—not a fact. Encourage students to discuss the topic with their families, with friends, and in other organizations they may

belong to. Stating your opinion may arouse the wrath of parents. Marc approaches such questions by stating that his role is not to influence but to present both sides of an issue as objectively as possible. He tries to steer the class into a discussion among students that will present both sides of a topic. His purpose is to instigate thinking so students may explore their own values and draw their own conclusions. Because your district may have a policy concerning such matters, be prepared to check with your building principal before you begin potentially controversial discussions. Your district should provide printed copies of such policies.

If a student asks a general question in a way and at a time that you feel is appropriate, feel free to answer if you wish to do so. "Yes, I'm married." "No I don't have children at home because I have 23 wonderful ones right here at school." Do not give any response you would not want to see printed on a billboard. Definitely do not answer anything that could get you fired. You can rest assured that anything you say will be repeated at one or more family dinner tables.

If you are asked a question and you don't know the answer, it's better to say you don't know than to make something up. You would hate to have to follow up on something like that.

PROFESSIONALISM AND YOUR COLLEAGUES

Giving Support

A term that's often tossed around in the workforce is "team player." While logic might dictate that such a person is perceived as a helper, how do you know the difference between a team player and a doormat?

Team players can be counted on to help, yet not to be taken advantage of. If an emergency requires that a colleague leave school and you're asked to cover a class, do so if possible. There may be a time when you must make such a request. If a coach is short of timers for a track meet and you have no other obligations, it's a good idea to help out. Teaching is an isolated profession, and it's easy to remain in your own comfortable niche. Helping other teachers gives you a broader perspective on your school.

However, if the same people keep asking, and you seem to be the only person sacrificing prep time, evenings, and weekends, don't be afraid to say, "I'm afraid that I won't be able to help out this time." Your own stress level is critical. The important thing is to participate to the extent that you meet other people and help out when you can.

In the turmoil of the workday, people often forget to thank their fellow workers. Many people in a school building work to make our jobs easier. Don't forget these people. Say "Thank you." An occasional note, card, or small gift will be appreciated. The day after Mary, a secondary reading teacher, covered a class for a colleague, she arrived at school to find a note and a rose on her desk. You don't need to shower your colleagues with gifts, but being appreciated and remembered goes a long way in building a relationship.

A strong correlation exists between how your colleagues perceive you and how your students do. The whiner who perpetually complains to coworkers is often the dark cloud in a student's day. If your fellow teachers regard you as a competent professional, they will treat you with respect. Students will notice this and will be inclined to treat you respectfully.

Life in the Public Eye

Kathy, a sixth grade teacher, tells a story about a Saturday some time ago when she had been teaching for two years. She'd been scrambling that day, like most people who work outside the home, to grocery shop, pick up her prescription from the pharmacy, and grab clothes from the cleaners.

While rolling her cart down the aisle at the supermarket, Kathy encountered one of her students, his younger brother, and his mother. She'd met this mother during conferences, but suddenly Kathy panicked. She worried about how she was dressed. She was wearing well-worn jeans and her sorority sweatshirt; her hair was carelessly pulled back in a ponytail. Next, she became acutely aware of the contents of her cart—two six-packs of beer and a large bottle of wine—which she saw her student, his brother, and his mother eyeing. Kathy didn't think about the chicken, apples, lettuce, foil, and canned corn that were also in the cart; her thoughts focused solely on the beer and wine.

She chatted for a few minutes with the family, but remained uncomfortably aware of her cart's contents and berated herself for not being better dressed. Another embarrassment occurred when Kathy later handed her prescription for birth control pills to the pharmacist. As the pharmacist typed the label he began to make conversation. "It's great the amount of canned food your class was able to collect for the food bank this year. You must be really proud." In a wave of cold realization, Kathy recognized the father of one of her students.

Kathy was beginning to realize that teachers live in a fishbowl. Even though she knew she'd done nothing wrong, she still felt uncomfortable about what the parents might have assumed. She knew that if she wanted to stay in teaching, she either needed to adjust to the reality of living in her community as a semipublic figure or find other ways to deal with her private life. The degree to which you are faced with these types of situations will depend on the size of your community and your living proximity to where you teach. You can just never tell when you will see someone who calls, "Oh, there's Jenny's teacher!"

Similarly, if you choose to become active in a community group, you must never lose sight of your image as a professional educator in the community. The general public is all too quick to find fault with teachers and to use a single instance to condemn the whole lot of us. Because we are entrusted with the minds of youngsters, we often have to present public profiles that are on the squeaky-clean side.

Working Hours

Another aspect of life in the public eye is your working hours. Parents know that you work during school time, but they don't see you grading papers, planning lessons, preparing labs, and making models. People are not aware that during the summer teachers go to school themselves, are employed, and travel or study to enhance their curricula. Don't apologize or engage in a debate about the time you spend working. You don't want to be perceived by your students or other staff members as someone who beats the kids out the door. Just realize that you are in the public eye on this issue too. As more schools become year-round and develop alternative schedules this may diminish as an area of concern, but for the time being it is something else to think about.

PROFESSIONAL ORGANIZATIONS AND CONFERENCES

Professional organizations are groups who associate for the purpose of support and improving teaching. A great many teachers choose to join a general teacher's association. These organizations are usually structured to include a local, state, and national affiliation. Two examples are the National Education Association and the American Federation of Teachers. A teachers' association can provide a wide variety of services to its members. It may engage in collective bargaining to obtain a suitable master contract covering all teachers in the district. It may also provide you with the best possible insurance packages, provide legal support, and advise you if your contractual rights are not being respected. The national association may offer additional insurance coverage to educators.

Whether you join such an organization is a personal preference in most districts, but you will find that the benefits are worth the price of dues. A foreign language teacher was sued recently over a conflict with a student who had cheated on a semester exam. The parents said that the teacher had destroyed their daughter's 4.0 grade point average, thereby ruining her reputation for life. The association lawyer met with the teacher, and the ensuing litigation did not cost the teacher a penny.

Another type of teaching organization is the subject area group. These associations function on the local, state, national, and international level. They exist to advance members' knowledge and teaching expertise in a particular subject area. Membership includes a subscription to a publication that features articles on philosophies, how-to lessons, and successful classroom experiences. These articles are usually written by teachers and provide a fresh look and a boost when you are feeling overwhelmed by your teaching load. Joining the organization and receiving the journals are the easy part; finding time to read them is the hard part. Set up a specific time to read. You could set aside one lunch a week to spend some time reading professional journals. Read your journals during silent reading in your class for ten minutes every day, or sit and have a cup of coffee and read one morning each week.

Most associations sponsor yearly state, regional, national, and international conferences and conventions. The conventions include publisher and supplier displays, seminar meetings, workshops, and well-known speakers. It is a chance to see what is new on the market, to hear some new thoughts and ideas, and to meet other people with similar interests. You will discover that teachers in other districts and states have experiences similar to yours. It is a chance to generate new ideas and possible solutions to problems you've encountered. The costs you incur while attending these conferences are tax-deductible, so save all of your receipts.

We all remember that the first years of teaching are lean times burdened by college debts, low salaries, and family obligations. However, we still recommend joining a professional organization. The information and support you gain are well worth the cost of membership.

RESEARCH

What?! On top of coping with curriculum, discipline, parents, colleagues, administrators, reports, and duty, this book dares to talk about research? Unbelievable! You probably won't have much time to do educational research in your first year or two of teaching. However, if you are working on a project or a night class, or just need more information on a method of effective teaching, others in your school might prove to be valuable resources. Your school librarian can tell you if there are any books or journals on the topic. Your principal, counselor, school psychologist, or resource room teacher might have articles that are just what you need.

CONCLUSION

Professionalism is demonstrated in dress, attitude, and communication. Maintaining this image requires common sense and discretion, both in and out of the classroom.

You enhance your professional growth when you join a professional organization, attend conferences, and read. A list of names and addresses of professional associations appears in the appendix at the end of this book. Write to those that interest you to inquire about membership and benefits.

chapter two

Classroom Management

Kristin Snyder

My advice for new teachers is to try to see things from the students' point of view. Teachers are already interested in what they're talking about, and they already know it — students want to be interested, and then, they'll want to know

New teachers, be open and honest with your students. It's also helpful to have a sense of humor. This way it will be easier to connect with your students, which makes it much simpler to earn their respect. If you have their respect, your life will be much easier.

Nikki Gustaveson

11

Mary, a secondary reading teacher, still remembers that tall, lanky troublemaker all these years later. Tom was towering past six feet and still growing, with a cheerful, teddy-bear face. He wasn't a bad kid—he just worked hard at constantly avoiding work that might accidentally result in learning. He was a low achiever and definitely not interested in taking a chance at being successful. The year seemed to stretch forever. Mary looked forward to the day when this nagging, whining senior would graduate.

Over the months, Mary had talked to Tom quietly, spoken sharply, yelled, threatened, and nagged—all the usual techniques. In one normal morning, everyone needed her simultaneously. Tom appeared at her desk again with yet another work-avoiding request. Mary found herself doing what education professors advise against: She pointed an accusing finger at Tom and started to shake it for emphasis. However, since Mary is 5 feet 6 inches, and Tom had long passed the 6-feet-6-inch mark, her imperious finger punctuated the air somewhere not too far below his chin. Suddenly she stood outside herself, saw the ludicrous situation in progress, and instinctively made the right decision.

Mary said, "Hey wait a minute. This isn't working." She pulled over her desk chair, climbed on the seat, and was a head above Tom. She wagged a finger down at his face. They broke into friendly laughter, both seeing the ridiculousness of the whole scene. That laughter created a feeling of mutual respect. From that day forward, Tom worked hard on every assignment. He brought Mary two yellow roses when he graduated.

Discipline is the scariest unknown for teachers. Our first question about students should *not* be: "How can I make them do what I want?" but rather "What do these students need to flourish?" Discipline plans need to have four main focus points. The plan must:

■ Address the safety and well-being of every student.

- Teach and model respect for self and others.
- Help students establish self-discipline.
- Encourage working together to solve problems.

Ultimately, all students can develop self-discipline. Classroom procedures should be structured to achieve these goals. You need to make the final decision about which of the techniques discussed in this book suit your teaching style and personality. Every teaching decision that you make in regard to discipline needs to be consistent and compassionate.

All teachers arrive in the classroom with a knowledge base, some teaching materials, and a sense of curriculum expectations, but with little or no clear idea about the personalities of the students and how they will mold into a functioning learning group. Getting to know those who occupy the desks is a monumental, creative job. Students will express their needs and deliberately or accidentally create the most unexpected dilemmas at the most unexpected times. The only guarantee is that the unexpected will happen—unexpectedly. Unfortunately, this beginning-of-the-year concern does not disappear after the first years of teaching. The first day of a classroom full of new students

Effective discipline for a tall student

and all the accompanying stress never changes. You just become more adept at the process of creating a positive learning climate. However, even as a first-year teacher, there are things you can do to create the classroom atmosphere you want right from the very beginning.

BEFORE THE FIRST DAY OF SCHOOL–GENERAL STANDARDS FOR MANAGEMENT

Before you step into your classroom, you'll want to have a clear idea in your mind about how you will approach most discipline problems. The following ideas can help you do this.

Avoiding Classroom Management Problems

A majority of the discipline problems that rear their ugly heads stem from students' need for attention or power. This is universal in all grades. You can do a lot to reduce or eliminate these types of problems.

1. Give lots of individual attention. The easiest way to accomplish this is to be at your door to greet students when they arrive. Do this whenever you can. It seems simple, but it produces great results. Barbara, a middle school language arts teacher, began greeting her students by name as they entered her classroom. The next test scores were ten points higher, even though she had done nothing else differently—she had only recognized each student individually each day.

2. When a student needs your attention, make it undivided. Hold up a hand, make quick eye contact, or give some other form of acknowledgement to a waiting student, and remain attentive to the first. When you have attended to that student, turn to the second and say, "Thank you for being patient. Now you have

my undivided attention." You might laugh and suggest taking numbers. Students will usually wait patiently if they know that they will get your attention. If you find yourself in the situation of having many students waiting for you all the time, examine how you are explaining activities and assignments. Providing directions both verbally and in writing may alleviate some of the individual questions you are met with each day.

3. When students are working at their desks, move among them and watch them work. Point out a phrase you like, answer questions, utter a quiet "Good job, Carl," or ask, "Are you doing okay? What can I help you with?" Every student can be confident that you will come by his or her desk several times. Students won't feel the need to sit with an arm waving in the air. They can keep working knowing that you will be there soon. Using proximity as a classroom management tool is a positive way to avoid problems. Moving closer to a developing situation reinforces the academic work that is being done while not giving more attention to the negative behavior.

4. Know that this positive attention is the easiest preventative measure you can take in the classroom. Students need lots of consistent, positive attention. As you get to know your students, tailor your responses to meet their needs. Some students need more reassurance than others.

5. Provide legitimate, specific praise. Recognize improvements and progress toward the desired goal. Acknowledge that the student is trying, and ask what the student will work on next.

6. Engage students in before- and after-class conversations. "So how was the soccer game last night?" Showing that you are aware of life outside the classroom may open up reserved students and communicate that you care about them as individuals.

Kathy encountered Wendy, an especially in-corrigible child, in her sixth grade classroom. She knew the child was acting out because of problems at home, but the disruptions hindered the other students, and Wendy was consistently being moved away from the other members of her group. Kathy knew that this student would benefit from frequent positive attention. She acknowledged appropriate behavior, correct answers, and positive interactions with other students.

At the end of two weeks, Kathy realized the student was acting out less frequently, and she pointed this out to Wendy. Kathy also noticed that when Wendy worked with math groups she would frequently act out. Kathy asked Wendy if she would feel more comfortable working alone on the assignment, thus giving Wendy control of the decision. Wendy made the move to work independently and the acting out stopped again.

Wendy's case illustrates the point that some children require a lot of teacher support and attention to avert or end behavior problems. Other students will require this degree of teacher interaction only at vulnerable times in their lives.

One difficulty with handling discipline problems in the classroom is that a minor irritation can mutate into a major difficulty before a teacher—especially a new teacher—even realizes something is wrong. Eventually you will become adept at spotting trouble before it happens. Your students may even ask if you are psychic. Don't answer. Only smile benevolently and knowingly.

There will be times when you are faced with more severe classroom management problems. These issues are discussed later in this chapter.

THE ADMINISTRATIVE PROCESS

Have a clear knowledge of the administrative process at your building or the district level for dealing with a disruptive student. If no one covers this specific topic in the first days before school begins, ask. Keep a copy of the written policy within easy reach. Ideally, you will want to handle all but extreme discipline problems yourself. By handling conflicts in a timely manner, you retain control of the situation and consistently demonstrate your leadership role in the classroom. The goal is to share the responsibility for control with the students, but you are the leader and must set the example. This active role as in-class leader is appropriate in the eyes of your administration and it adds to your teaching credibility. Students will respect your consistent, compassionate classroom management skills. The administration and support staff is there to help you if you need their assistance. Sending a student to the principal should be a last resort when the problem has escalated past what you feel capable of dealing with, you have already exhausted all other avenues, and the student's behavior has not changed.

TEACHER'S ROLE

Voice Control

Mentally put yourself through the discipline process. Think about what you will say. Rehearse in a calm, low-pitched voice. When your voice indicates you are angry, you will have a difficult time dealing with the student. Keeping your voice low and calm will demonstrate to the student that you are in control of the situation and that you are serious about the matter.

Consistency

Be consistent. This is the key to effective classroom management. In the beginning of the year you are not familiar with personalities. Use that to your advantage. Apply all expectations and rules to all students. Just as it is the behavior, not the student, you are attempting to change, it is your job to be fair and firm with all students. Do not become furious or overly frustrated. Send the message that the lesson is the most important thing.

Deal with disruptions in the least obtrusive way possible and continue with what you were doing.

Firmness

Be firm when disciplining. If a student comes tearfully to your desk after class with extenuating circumstances that explain the disruption, you might say, "I understand your situation and I am glad to know about it. However, you have to think about your behavior in class and show respect for the other students." This will convey that you care, but that you will continue applying rules consistently to the whole class.

Avoiding Academic Penalties

Do not use academic penalties for behavior problems. Nothing can turn kids off to writing quicker than the 500 word essay on "Why I Shouldn't Misbehave in Class." The same can be said for any subject area. Our job is to engage students and strive to help them become lifelong learners. Doing two extra pages of math problems sends a very confusing message.

Reasonable Consequences

If you've set up your expectations in the beginning and the students know the consequences for their actions, you have the advantage. Consequences should be reasonable and fit the offense. Having a student clean out his or her desk because he or she is unable to locate a textbook is a good example of this. It shows students that they are responsible for the materials that have been checked out to them and that you want to help them become more organized. However, students need to know about these consequences from the beginning of the year.

Special Services

Learn about the services your school may provide to students with special circumstances and severe behavioral problems. Read the chapters in this book on ancillary personnel, record keeping, and parents. A more detailed discussion of these services follows in Chapter 9 on Ancillary Personnel.

CLASSROOM RULES

Students need clear parameters. You may feel most comfortable determining these boundaries yourself. Another alternative is to allow your students the opportunity to help develop a set of rules that all can live with. This empowers students and helps them further develop feelings of confidence and self-control. Be clear about your own needs and expectations.

How to Use Classroom Rules

Here are some suggestions that you may find helpful in determining your classroom expectations.

1. Keep the rules simple and stated in a positive manner. For example, "Use appropriate language," rather than, "Don't swear."
2. Have logical, enforceable consequences. For example, if a student writes on a desk, he or she must take time to clean the desk.
3. Post the rules and the consequences.
4. Read and review the rules several times at the beginning of the semester and review throughout the year. Present the rules both verbally and in writing. Some teachers include questions about the rules in the first quiz.
5. Another idea is to include the rules in a homework assignment for students to share with parents.

You may choose to invest some class time discussing or writing about the rules. Students could role-play identifying and expressing their feelings about common school-related problems.

Brian, a social studies teacher, acknowledges to his classes that since students usually want to prove their maturity to the world, his class is a

CLASSROOM POLICIES

1. All rules identified in the school handbook apply in this room.
2. Arrive on time, ready to learn, with all necessary materials.
3. Be responsible for your own materials and workspace.
4. Be respectful of others' property and right to learn.

ASSIGNMENTS

1. Written work is due at the beginning of the period. All work must be turned in on hard copy unless otherwise specified.
2. Late work will be accepted up to two days after the due date. The grade will be dropped one letter grade for each day it is late. For example, a B paper, if turned in one day late, will earn a grade of C.
3. Your name, the date, the period, and the assignment must appear in the upper right-hand corner.

GRADING POLICY

1. Your grade will be calculated from your achievement in the following areas: tests, quizzes, lab work, your digital portfolio, and other assignments.
2. The following scale will be used:
   90%–100% = A
   80%–89% = B
   70%–79% = C
   60%–69% = D
   0%–59% = F
3. Your quarter grade will be determined by averaging all your grades from that quarter.
4. Your semester grade will be determined by averaging your quarter grades.

Ms. Smith
Breckenridge High School

perfect place to start. He goes on to explain that swearing is inappropriate. His class offers an opportunity to stretch language. "We all know what those words mean," he drawls in his sagest tone, "but in this class we practice speaking and writing about those feelings using subtle, more appropriate, tasteful words. You will impress your allies and frustrate your enemies."

Methods of Establishing Classroom Rules

Teacher-Established Rules   You may decide on your rules before your students arrive. Three general ones that work well might be:

1. Follow all published school rules. (This covers all school rules that need to be enforced to maintain a safe, positive school climate.)
2. Arrive in class on time and ready to work. (This covers all the nitty-gritty stuff such as pencil, paper, books, assignments the dog hasn't eaten, and a positive attitude.)
3. Treat all class members with respect and expect it in return. (This rule says the teacher and student deserve equal consideration. It also covers the student who sleeps in class, because sleeping is definitely disrespectful.)

ELEMENTARY CLASSROOM RULES

- Show respect for yourself, your classmates, and our school.
- Practice good conversation skills.
- Listen when others speak.
- Let people speak without interruption.
- Respond politely.
- Respect others' ideas.
- Take care of your possessions.

Student-Established Rules You might decide to involve students in establishing rules. It's a good idea to begin your lesson on classroom rules by discussing etiquette and traditional codes of behavior. Include the origin of these rules and why we have them. On the first day of class, Brian assigns the following homework: "For tomorrow, write five classroom rules and be ready to discuss and turn them in." Because it is the beginning of the year, excitement about school is still high and most students will return with homework in hand. This affords Brian the chance to award each student a good homework grade and sends a strong message about student involvement. The class period is used to discuss the suggested rules, and the class reaches consensus on the list. The rules are generally consistent from class to class, and the consequences are often more severe than Brian would have planned, but the students follow them because *they* established them.

The procedure is the same for elementary students. Kathy, who teaches sixth grade, has her students establish rules during class meetings. She thinks the process teaches important communication skills while empowering students. Students can brainstorm possible rules with parents for a homework assignment. The following day each student shares the ideas from home and the class decides which rules they want to adopt and live with for the year.

Safety Rules If you are responsible for a class using a laboratory setting (science, consumer technology, industrial technology, or physical education) you need to establish specific safety-related rules in order to provide a safe learning environment. While students may help create the policies about getting along, rules concerning safety must be made by the teacher and must be strictly enforced.

ADMINISTERING CONSEQUENCES

The following is a sample of a possible discipline policy. Become aware of the discipline steps established by your school or district. If you don't follow the procedure, you may find that legally your administration will not be able to support you. You will be instructed to return to your classroom with the disruptive student and begin documenting the behavior. Make a note of each step in that student's file.

1. First offense: Issue a nonverbal warning. This might be in the form of a meaningful look, a tapping on the student's desk, or moving over in the direction of the disruptive student. When you are addressing the whole class and off-topic conversation continues between students, you might move between the talkers. Proximity is an excellent classroom management technique. You may pause mid sentence and stare passively until the talking stops. Then continue your sentence. In turn, do not interrupt when a student is speaking. If the chatter resumes, stop again and go to step 2.

2. Second offense: Issue a verbal warning. You might couple a simple, "Tom!" with a nonverbal action and return to the lesson quickly. Depending on the student, this contact could be made quietly, one-to-one. This shows that you expect compliance. If the student still misbehaves, go to step 3.

3. Third offense: Have a conference after class or during a break. "Tom, I asked you to please listen. Please see me after class." And continue with the lesson. It is crucial that you do not argue the point with the student in front of the class. Doing so will allow the conflict to overshadow the learning and puts you in the

position of having to exert power over the student. Begin the conference with a statement like, "I'm glad that we could get together to talk now. It was not appropriate at the time to discuss what happened." Think about where you and the student will sit. If you sit at your desk, the implication of authority remains. Consider sitting at a table or in student desks. If the student refuses to sit, accept that and either casually stand or lean on the desktop so you and the student will still occupy the same level of space.

Give the student an opportunity to express his or her version. When the student is finished, pause a few seconds thoughtfully. Then paraphrase the essence of the student's response. Identify the conflict or problem as you see it. If the student interrupts you, wait politely and say in a calm voice, "I didn't interrupt you when you were giving your version. I need the same respect from you. May I finish?" Mutually generate possible alternatives, evaluate the possible courses of action, and decide on the best solution. Make sure the student understands the established consequence if the behavior continues. End the conference with a statement of your confidence in the student's ability to implement the solution. You will usually not have to go beyond this step. However, if the misbehavior continues, go to step 4.

4. Inform the parents. This can be done through a phone call, a note, or a conference. State the facts. Tell the parent the steps you've taken so far. "Amy is in my class and I've called you because I need you to know about this situation." Ask for the parent's help and support in reinforcing acceptable behavior. You need to follow up this contact with a call to update the same parent on the situation. This will serve as reinforcement to the student. Keep a written, dated record of the conversation. Use dis-

cretion in leaving phone messages. If you are returning a call, it may be appropriate to leave a message. However, initiating contact with a parent by leaving a message may have more drastic results than you had anticipated. Parents may never receive your message or they might assume the worst. If needed, proceed to the next step.

5. Inform the counselor. The counselor might be able to provide insight into the behavior of the student. A meeting with the counselor may or may not include you and might result in an increased understanding on both sides. This same counselor could initiate special services for the student if the situation warrants.

6. Write a referral to the person responsible for discipline in your school. In this referral, state the problem clearly and list the steps you have taken to try and solve the problem. If you have to write a referral, use short concise sentences. Report, don't editorialize. Take a few minutes to read over what you have written. If you are angry or overly frustrated, take some time and reread the referral later. Make another draft if you find you did not include important details. Make a copy of the referral and put it in a secure place. The administrator may meet with the student, establish a plan, and inform you and the parents of conference results.

Repeated problems might result in the student's being removed from your class or taking part in a support program in which she or he can function successfully. If you must work through these steps with a student, keep written records of the process. Be sure these documents are not in a place where other students or parents can view them. Many of the new electronic grade book programs allow you to keep anecdotal records. This would be an excellent place to record student behavior conferences and parent contacts.

Extreme Violations

District policies are generally in place to support the teacher after all discipline strategies have been utilized and found ineffective. Examples of extreme disciplinary violations might include continuous insubordination, verbal or physical abuse, or possession of a controlled substance or weapon.

Steps in this a disciplinary process for extreme violations might include:

- **First Violation:** The student is sent to the administrator for a conference, and the parents are notified by phone or in writing. The teacher submits paperwork on the incident. Some form of suspension might be initiated, depending on the severity of the incident. Many school districts have a zero tolerance policy concerning weapons. If you feel that it may escalate the situation by requesting that the student go to see an administrator, notify the office that you need help by sending a reliable student, using your call box, or telephone. See Chapter 7 on emergencies.
- **Second Violation:** The student's parents are called to set up a conference with the administrator. The counselor, student, and teacher may or may not be involved in this meeting. Many teachers prefer having the student at this meeting because the student is then able to tell his or her side firsthand and to take responsibility for the actions. Written records of the conference are sent to all parties concerned and some form of suspension might be initiated.
- **Third and Subsequent Violations:** If this is the student's third offense, a formal suspension might be initiated if all parties deem that there have been inadequate attempts at improvement. The student is often referred to the hearing panel of the school district and may be moved to another school or face suspension for the remainder of the semester or school year.

Elementary School—
Special Considerations

Since elementary teachers work with the same students all day, there are opportunities for more in-depth discussions about behavior. It is important to develop a rapport and sense of trust with the students. Frequently, a student in tears over a situation needs to gain control before you can talk. You may need to leave the child alone to regain composure. You might offer comfort, but don't try to deal with the student who is upset. You may find that the child becomes frenzied instead of working toward solving the problem.

When the child is ready to talk, use "I" statements: "I feel . . . (feeling) because (context) . . . I can't . . . (barrier) and I want to . . . (goal)." State that the inappropriate behavior is not respectful. "I would like to talk with you about what you did, not about what Bob did to you." Don't allow the child to reduce the situation to "But she told me to." Try to get the child to identify his or her own actions and feelings.

Robert, an elementary teacher, relates a story about a group of five girls in his second/third grade classroom. Because there was an odd number in the group, one was always feeling left out. The left-out girl (not always the same one) would come to Robert in tears, complaining. The girls were often upset; mean words were exchanged. Even though the class held several meetings about friendship, the problem remained unresolved.

One recess, Robert kept all five girls in the room. He reminded them that each of them had expressed hurt feelings and that they all wanted to be friends. He asked them to think about the discussions they'd had in class, their own feelings, and what they would like to have happen in this situation. He told them to talk about their problem and to let him know their proposed solutions. Later, they told Robert they had talked about each of them being bossy to the others and then feeling left out. They decided to think about each person getting a turn to decide what to do, and if they felt left out, each of them would join in and not whine about it. When the girls stated their feelings and what they wanted, they became good mutual friends.

Later in the year, a school counselor was talking with the least secure of the five girls and remarked that her friendships this year seemed stronger. The student reported that the meeting the five girls had held together was most important to her. The girls had learned to respect each other by stating their own feelings and identifying the problem.

Individual Considerations

When a discipline problem occurs in your classroom, remember that the student is not making a personal attack on you. These kinds of problems often arise because of frustration with the task at hand, need for attention, stress from an out-of-class conflict, or fatigue. Over the years you will become wiser about the reasons for these types of problems.

When a problem with a student does occur—and it will—stay calm. This will take practice. Most of the time you will be able to follow your established procedure, like the one outlined above.

A quiet moment with a student

However, you need to recognize all students as unique, and you may need to expand for some students. You could try these ideas:

- Think about what you are going to do.
- Take a deep breath and exhale slowly. It will help you regain some control and send the message that you are going to deal with the problem in a rational manner.
- Keep your voice pitch low and speak slowly.
- The first time a student presents a problem, begin by following your standard procedure. Issuing a nonverbal warning is usually a good first step.
- Avoid reprimanding a student in front of other classmates. This creates a power struggle and is demeaning to the student.

Consistently follow your behavior management plan. This will help establish your credibility.

Recently, a colleague who teaches special needs students did not follow this advice. What she did is an example of what won't work. It was early in the year, and the teacher was still getting to know the students. They were working on an assignment, and as the teacher walked around the room she discovered one young man sitting slouched, arms crossed, staring into space. She told him calmly to get to work. He didn't answer. After several requests and no action she changed her request to a choice: "You can either get to work or you can go to the office." She offered the choice several times in as calm a voice as she could muster. Eventually, the student used abusive language, and the teacher had to withdraw her choices and send him to the office. By this time, the entire class was focused on the conflict and not the assignment.

This teacher made the following errors:

1. She had not followed her standard behavior management procedure. Sending the boy to

the office did not solve the class problem. The assignment was never completed, and the boy slumped back to class the following day.

2. The student had been put on the defensive. She had given him an impossible choice without giving him an opportunity to explain his side of the story or show improvement.

3. The student was put on the spot in front of his peers. Everyone in this situation lost.

Instead, this teacher could have done the following:

1. She could have quietly asked if there was anything she could do to help the student or why he wasn't working.

2. She could have listened, then suggested that the student stop by and talk further after class.

3. She could have reminded the student of the directions and the amount of time remaining in class for completing the work.

4. She could have checked back with him frequently and reinforced any approximations toward work.

This incident is an example of expanding the verbal warning step to accommodate individual needs. If the problem is one you feel a support person can help solve, solicit advice. Chapter 9 further explains the role of these support personnel.

Your job is to teach students, not to solve their personal problems. That sounds hard-hearted, but all too often teachers who genuinely care become entangled in the personal lives of students and end up in ethically or legally difficult positions. Students may use up your compassion to enable their own inappropriate behaviors. Recognize their individual differences, discipline them with consistency, and, if necessary, send them to personnel trained to handle student advocacy.

GROUP BEHAVIOR MANAGEMENT

If the problem is affecting the entire class, you could try these steps:

- Stop the lesson and identify the problem. If it is something that you can deal with, do so: The room may be too stuffy, the overhead is not focused, the tracking on the VCR needs adjusting, or the entire class did not understand the directions.
- If the problem is major, you may want to call a class meeting. "What can we do about people blurting out their ideas and not letting others participate?" When you have reached consensus on possible solutions, restart the lesson.
- If the problem affecting the lesson is out of your control and doesn't affect your class (across the hall Mr. M has a dog in his room), shut your door, lead your class in a relaxation exercise, or laugh about it, then refocus on the lesson and proceed.

Fights

If a confrontation between students escalates to a full-fledged fight, you need to be ready to make some fast decisions. These decisions depend on your school policy concerning fights. When a fight begins:

- Try to separate the fighters by *verbal* persuasion. Remain calm. The other students may be frightened or excited. Say in a commanding voice, "Syd, please come with me." Repeat several times. Use the students' names if possible. Keep repeating statements that may discourage the fighting: "Chris, break it up!" "Pat, this isn't going to solve anything!"
- Send a student to get other adult help.

- Think carefully before you step between the fighters. A lot depends on how big they are and the circumstances. The students may be armed. Your proximity is critical, but you do not want to endanger yourself.
- If no help arrives, send another student for support.

Laughter and Humor

Laughter is a highly desirable part of positive discipline, but it can be elusive, difficult to control, and fragile. There is the laughter that ripples through the classroom when everyone shares a pun or a joke that presents itself in the lesson. There is the joke a teacher uses to focus a topic or complete an idea. A teacher exercising a good sense of humor can adjust to all the unexpected changes that occur in the school day. Try not to let all the daily disruptions cause you undue stress. Shrug your shoulders mentally, handle the important items, and move on.

Making fun of a student or another teacher is never appropriate. Laughing at a student's mistakes is intolerable. Certain student behaviors may seem distracting. The behaviors exhibited at eight or ten years of age may seem inappropriate but are a part of that person's temperament and will be a big part of his or her adult personality. The student who always has one more idea to share or the student who is slow and methodical need not be viewed as a problem. The child who picks up on your every error may be a future research scientist. A sense of humor will allow you to respect individual differences while keeping your sanity intact.

We are not all funny and exciting twenty-four hours a day every day, so don't feel as if you need to be. Be yourself. Just keep in mind that not everything that happens is earth-shattering. Expressions of humor and looking on the light side can help prevent classroom management problems.

Dealing with Student Humor

When you tell jokes in the classroom or something humorous is in the curriculum, your students will want to tell jokes. Be prepared for the inappropriate stories. Sometimes it seems as if students don't know any other kind; unfortunately, many kids don't know what is appropriate and not.

The humor of some younger students is often hard to understand. A phrase that reduces them to giggles can sound like an ordinary sentence to you. Be prepared to not understand. The students may feel the same way when they hear your adult jokes.

Robert has a cartoon in his classroom: A caveman is standing at the chalkboard writing, "I will not act primitive in class." One day Robert listened while one of his third graders tried to explain to another why the cartoon was funny. Understanding humor and cartoons requires cognitive abilities and higher levels of thinking.

When a student wants to tell a joke, ask if the joke contains offensive language, pertains to the lesson, or will embarrass anyone in class. You might ask, "Can everyone's parents sit in this room and watch without being offended?" Another way to handle jokes is to ask students to tell them to you before or after class. After you've heard the joke, you can determine if it is appropriate for class.

Sarcasm

When you are tired or overwhelmed, that next question can put you over the edge and solicit a sarcastic response. The student may well deserve every prick of your barbed remark, but don't say it. Bite your tongue. Sarcasm, condescending behavior, and rude remarks have no place in the classroom and destroy the positive climate you've been working so hard to establish. If you treat your students with dignity and respect, most will treat you with dignity in return.

CONCLUSION

Although each discipline problem is unique, common sense should dictate your actions. Consider each student as an individual. Being clear and consistent with your expectations and the established classroom rules from the very beginning will go a long way toward establishing a positive environment. Advise students of the consequences and then follow through. Following through is difficult, but it is crucial. A teacher who is fair, firm, and consistent, and maintains a sense of humor is way ahead of the game.

The Classroom

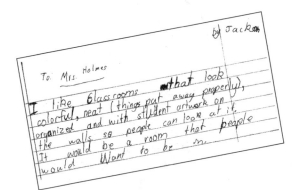

by Jackson

To: Mrs. Holmes

I like classrooms that look colorful, neat (things put away properly), organized and with student artwork on the walls so people can look at it. It would be a room that people would want to be in.

BEFORE THE FIRST DAY

To help set the tone for a successful year, it's important to organize your room before the students ever enter. "Decorate" the room and decide whether you wish to determine the class rules or allow your students to create them. Make sure your desk contains the supplies you'll need and that you have, to the best of your knowledge, the texts, reference books, hardware, software, and teaching materials that you'll need to get started.

If you are a new teacher in a school, you've probably attended some orientation meetings already. It's a good idea to "scope out" your room as soon as possible. The principal, department chair, or another teacher might help you find your room, obtain a key, and begin the organization of your classroom.

While you're in your building, acquaint yourself with the other facilities you'll probably be using. Locate the media center and ask about the procedures for checking out materials and bringing your students for research. Find the counselors' offices. Locate the room where the AV equipment is kept. Will you be sharing VCRs and TVs with other teachers? What is the procedure for checking these out? Will your computer be situated so that a PC-to-TV cable can easily reach the monitor?

Your school will probably have a cafeteria and teachers' lounge. Locate these, as well as restrooms. The more organized you are and able to find your way around that first day, the better.

Daily Schedule

Scheduling is one area where elementary and secondary schools differ, since elementary teachers plan for a whole day with diverse subjects. The middle school or secondary teacher plans for one-hour periods or two-hour blocks, for subjects that are taught more than once during the day.

Usually, before the first day of school, you will have a general idea of what the daily schedule will look like. The preliminary teachers' meetings advise you of times for beginning and ending the school day, breaks, lunch, and other special classes that students attend. For elementary people, it's important to consider when specialists in physical education, music, computer science, reading, art, math, speech, and other areas will meet with your students. Using this information, you can create a spreadsheet of your daily schedule (Chart 1). You can also make a weekly schedule, noting special classes and time slots (Charts 2 and 3, pages 38 and 39). This will probably change, but creating an initial outline will provide a place to start. You might try setting up several hypothetical schedules.

Chart 1

Example of Daily Schedule for Kindergarten—Outline

8:30 | 9:00	Opening Exercises	-Attendance -Calendar -Songs -Read to Class	12:15 | 12:45
9:00 | 9:30	Free Choice Activities		12:45 | 1:15
9:30 | 10:10	Language Arts Activities Math Activities		1:15 | 1:55
10:10 | 10:30	Outside Play		1:55 | 2:15
10:30 | 11:00	Special Unit Activities		2:15 | 2:45
11:00 | 11:15	Closing - Stories or Songs		2:45 | 3:00

Chart 2

Example of Weekly Schedule for Elementary—Outline

	8:30–10:10		10:30–11:40		12:25–1:30		1:50–3:00
Monday	Opening Jobs from helper chart Sharing Read to class	Writers' workshop	Math		Spelling Journals Pleasure reading		Science Social studies Health
Tuesday		Centers	Math		Computer lab		Science Social studies Health 2:25–2:55 Music
Wednesday		Centers	Math		Spelling Journals 12:55–1:25 Music		Science Social studies Health
Thursday		Math	Spelling Journals 11:00–11:30 P.E.		Writers' Workshop		Art
Friday		Writers' workshop	10:30–11:00 Library Spelling Journals		Centers		1:55–2:20 P.E. Small group games

(Column dividers labeled: 10:10–10:30 AM Recess | 11:40–12:25 Lunch | 1:30–1:50 PM Recess)

During the first weeks of school you should find one that works best. This scheduling and planning process is time-consuming but important. These and pacing are among the most crucial elements for success in the classroom.

Classroom Policies

The expectations you set for your students and your ability to be consistent about them are probably the most critical aspects of your teaching year. Although the cliche, "Don't smile until Christmas," sounds archaic and even inhumane,

Chart 3

Example of Weekly Schedule for Elementary

	Monday	Tuesday	Wednesday	Thursday	Friday
8:30–9:00	Opening Jobs from helper chart Sharing	Opening	Opening	Opening	Opening
9:00–10:10	Writers' workshop	Centers	Centers	Math	Writers' workshop
10:10–10:30	Recess	Recess	Recess	Recess	Recess
10:30–11:40	Math	Math	Math	Spelling Journals P.E. 11:00–11:30	Library 10:30–11:00 Spelling Journals
11:40–12:25	Lunch	Lunch	Lunch	Lunch	Lunch
12:25–1:30	Read to class Spelling Journals Pleasure reading	Read to class Spelling Journals Pleasure reading	Read to class Spelling Journals Computer lab	Read to class Writers' workshop	Read to class Centers
1:30–1:50	Recess	Recess	Recess	Recess	Recess
1:50–3:00	Social studies, Science, or Health	Social studies, Science, or Health	Social studies, Science, or Health	Art	P.E. 1:55–2:25 Games with small groups

the idea of beginning the year with a serious, solid foundation is not.

As a beginning teacher, it is difficult to set standards when you're not even sure what they are. Through the years, you learn which rules to carve in stone and which ones to toss. Refer to Chapter 2 for some lists of common expectations teachers have of students. Use your own personality to communicate the guidelines you choose to follow. You may wish to post them, incorporate them in an introductory handout, or state them verbally. Your introductory sheet might also state your teaching philosophy and include a course outline or syllabus. On the first or second day of school, review the handout with your students. Seeing and hearing your expectations should emphasize their importance. The most critical aspect of rule setting is your ability to *remain consistent and follow through.*

Classroom Procedures

The following are some topics and questions you will need to ponder before the first day of school. Some of these situations apply only to elementary, and some are applicable to middle and secondary grades as well.

Procedure for Entering Class   Where and how do you want your class to assemble before school and after breaks? If you have an outside door into your classroom, the students may be able to assemble there. If not, ask neighboring teachers what they do and if your class has an assigned spot. The advantage of a line of students is that you can greet each child first thing in the morning, after breaks, and provide a calming word as each child enters the classroom. There is a direct correlation between how students enter the classroom and how they conduct themselves while in that room. If they are calm when they enter the classroom, you save time and energy for more important tasks. Your goal is for students to enter enthusiastically, but respectfully. They need to know that running, punching, yelling, grabbing, and whining are not tolerated.

Some schools do not encourage students to enter the building before the first bell in the morning. Other schools allow students entry as soon as they arrive. If you find yourself in the latter situation, you will have an opportunity to spend a bit of relaxed time with your students before class. On the other hand, excluding students from the building before school provides additional planning time and eliminates some supervisory duties. With this arrangement, it's important to greet your students soon after the bell signals the beginning of the school day.

Storing Personal Belongings   Where will students keep their coats, lunches, and personal belongings? Secondary students usually have lockers where they can store their things. In elementary situations you will, most likely, have a coat closet or a set of coat hooks. If not, arrange for each student to have a place to keep his or her things. Large ice-cream tubs, boxes, plastic crates, and homemade wooden cubicles provide space to hold student belongings. Classrooms are seldom large enough for students to keep all their possessions around them without someone tripping over a coat or backpack. Some students, if permitted, would happily surround themselves with many treasured belongings, and must be reminded often that the collection can be hazardous. Younger students enthusiastically bring things from home to share with the class. Allowing and encouraging this shows that you value students as individuals and acknowledges that they have a life outside of school. However, require that they store these items in a central place, class museum, or backpack. This also helps alleviate the distractions that "shares" can cause during class.

Bringing Personal Treasures to Class   What kinds of personal belongings will you encourage students to bring? Encouraging them to bring items or share thoughts about what you are currently studying makes the curriculum more meaningful for them. There may be an established policy regarding bringing personal items to school. Check on this.

Many disruptions occur when students bring personal belongings to school. No matter what the district, school, or class policy is, students will attempt to bring "toys." Allowing elementary students to share stories, pets, or tales of adventure at designated times may help to alleviate problems.

Middle and high school students bring portable stereo equipment, skateboards, designer clothing, and other electronic gadgets to class rather than risk locker theft. Most policies state that school is not an appropriate place for expensive items. However, if a student brings such an item to class, have the student place the object out of sight, in a place that will not cause disruption. Remind the student that you cannot be responsible for the article and that he or she should not bring the item back. If the student persists in bringing "toys" that cause disruption, refer to Chapter 2 on disciplinary procedures.

Many students' most rewarding pieces of writing are about their pets. Bringing pets to share makes them tangible for everyone. Yet some teachers would never be comfortable with a rat or snake in the room, no matter how gentle these animals are reputed to be. Request that students bring any "live share" in a cage. If the animal can't spend the day in confinement, an adult who can take it home after share time must accompany it.

Collecting Notes and Money, Taking Attendance, and Lunch Count   How will you handle the daily tasks of lunch count, attendance, and note or money collection? For most situations a rotating helper schedule and chart takes care of daily routines. You may allow a student to fill out the attendance sheet if *you* double-check it.

Some teachers choose to do these tasks primarily themselves because it brings student attention to the teacher and prepares the students to attend to the following learning tasks. Other teachers instruct students in how to perform these duties. This allows the teacher the freedom to attend to the individual needs of students and parents. This emphasizes responsibility and reinforces a school-to-work skill. While the attendance taker is working, all other students complete their own assigned classroom tasks. This may be some daily math practice, silent reading, or another task that requires each person's full attention.

After being greeted at the door, Mike's students know to hand Mike any notes from home, store all other personal belongings in their cubbies, and then go directly to the carpeted group area in the front of the room. Mike places all the notes from his students in one place on his desk to be read and sorted as soon as possible. Any note that may demand his immediate attention can be quickly scanned as the child hands it to him. Mike then joins his students at the front of the room to take attendance, go over the daily schedule, make announcements, and perform a daily calendar routine as a part of the math curriculum. Mike's goal is to gather all the students together and focus their attention on the day's learning objectives. As soon as the students are engaged in their own activities, Mike sorts through the notes, checking off returned project money (all students need to return this, so Mike keeps a checklist), and files the notes accordingly. Mike makes memos in his own plan book detailing information from the notes that he needs to remember.

Ellen has designed a system for attendance and lunch count that her students monitor independently. Ellen also greets her student as they arrive. She collects notes, money, and homework. Students take care of their own personal belongings and move their own nametags to the designated spot that says, "I brought my lunch," or "I am having school lunch." The person who is responsible for attendance and lunch count that day then notes absences, tardies, and how many people want school lunch. That monitor reports this information to the office and the cafeteria manager. In Ellen's school this is done through e-mail. During this time, Ellen reads through the notes, sorts and files them if necessary, makes memos to herself in her plan book, checks off who has returned homework, checks with the attendance monitor, and deals with any individual questions or needs. At the same time, the remaining students are busy with the math challenge of the day. As they complete this task they are free to select related math games. Fifteen minutes later the entire class is ready to go over the daily math challenge and begin learning the new math concept.

Heading Papers　How will you require that students head their papers? This sounds like a trivial matter, but if you are suddenly faced with 155 papers, it is much easier to sort and record them if students use some uniform type of heading. It is much easier for you and your students if you let them know what you want from the beginning. Make a poster or demonstrate on the TV monitor so that all students may refer to the model as needed. On the first or second day, explain how and why papers need to be headed. Model this for the first few times until most of the students have the general idea mastered.

In the primary grades, just getting students to remember to put their names on papers is a major task. Later, you may want to include subject, date, page number, number of problems, and class period.

Robert assigns each student a number corresponding to the line his or her name occupies in his electronic grade book. As students turn in their work, Robert puts their papers in numerical order. It is then easy for him to identify any missing assignments.

Individuals Leaving the Classroom　How often and for what reason will you allow students to leave your classroom? Keeping interruptions to a minimum is important. Every student will occasionally need to use the rest room, sharpen a pencil, get a drink, or check out a library book during class time. Check to see if your school has a policy concerning students leaving class. Strongly urge students to get drinks, go to the rest room, sharpen pencils, or get supplies from lockers during break times. A useful, general rule is that only one person may be out of the room at any one time—assuming that it is necessary and you are not giving directions to the whole group. You might have one pass, such as a laminated piece of paper or object for out-of-class business, which may be used for temporary absences from class; this ensures that only one person is out of the room at a time. If students abuse the privilege, then the offender or whole class might lose this right. Explain this to the class ahead of time; it has a lasting impression. Barbara had a young man who seemed to need to use the rest room during her class at almost the same time each day. She had a suspicion that he was meeting another student in the hall. After about a week, she talked with the young man privately after class. In a serious tone she stated, "Rick, I've noticed that you seem to be needing to be excused quite often. Do you think there might be some medical problem that we should discuss with your parents and the nurse?" Rick gave Barbara a blank stare and mumbled a few words. The "visits" stopped.

Listing Student Supplies   How do you know what supplies the students need to bring? In most cases, if it is your first assignment, you will use what your predecessor asked students to bring. Keep a wish list in your plan book or in a special file so you can make these requests the next year. The supplies you need and require will change as your teaching style and curriculum needs do. For example, next year you may want all your students to have a three-ring notebook or plan book. You may want colored folders as portfolios. Other items on a student supply list might include pencils, pens, computer disks, markers, crayons, paper, erasers, glue, ruler, scissors, tissue, watercolor paints, lined paper, and folders. Your list may vary from school to school, grade to grade, and community to community. In some schools or districts, students pay a fee that covers all materials and activities for the year.

Room Environment Brian, a social studies teacher, has created a room that epitomizes an inviting classroom. An adept gardener, Brian has filled his windowsills with begonias and geraniums, a fern or two, and even an azalea. Student mobiles dangle like wind chimes, and posters and student projects wallpaper the room. Not that your classroom needs to look like an art gallery, zoo, or florist shop. But your classroom is an extension of you—it's your office and other home. Although some teachers don't wish their students to know one thing about them beyond the classroom, others feel differently. If you're an avid tennis player, backpacker, or musician, for example, you could hang posters that portray these activities. Your classroom should also be a place that reflects what your students are working on at the time. And whether it's stated in writing or suggested in photographs or paintings, your classroom should exhibit positive statements that encourage success and offer inspiration.

Katie teaches a middle school physical education class; she's a dedicated athlete and student of ballet. Her office and locker rooms display posters of gymnasts and dancers. A believer in wellness and self-discipline, Katie has created a working environment that models her philosophy and inspires her students.

Many teachers hang posters or photographs that suggest environmental awareness. You need, however, to practice sound judgment in what you display. Advertising certain values can be risky. Hanging a pro-life or pro-choice poster will probably result in a barrage of parental phone calls you don't need and an unsolicited visit from an administrator.

It's important that students feel comfortable and welcome in your classroom. Seeing their own work displayed provides them with a sense of pride and ownership. They also enjoy seeing pictures of themselves at work. For example, next to her posters, Katie hangs photographs of her volleyball players in action. Students appreciate seeing themselves stretching for that perfect spike or set. It's critical, too, that *you* feel comfortable, and that your room—your office—is a place you enjoy coming to each day.

When you enter your new classroom for the first time, it may look desolate and bare. Don't panic. It will take time to make the room your own. Robert inherited an elementary school classroom containing student desks and chairs in assorted sizes and conditions, a teacher's desk with no "big" chair to match, a pre–World War I world map, closets with some tired and faded bulletin board decorations, a box of recycled computer paper, several editions of assorted textbooks, and loads of empty space. Over the years he made and accumulated materials to fill the cupboards to be used for future units, but the walls and surroundings were still bare. Robert realized that the students could participate, and he suggested that they help decorate the classroom. The students pitched in enthusiastically.

Make things look ready for school, but not like the grand opening of the neighborhood stationery store. You do not need commercially produced materials to make your classroom inviting to students. Put up a few personal things; arrange your desk, computer, and printer. Make sure that, whether mounted in a cupboard or on a wall or placed on a cart, the TV monitor is positioned so that all students can see it. Arrange desks and learning centers. Leave a blank nametag or sheet of paper on each desk and prepare the walls for displaying student work. Some ideas for beginning-of-the-year bulletin boards include:

- a daily or weekly schedule
- a "Welcome to Students" sign or poster with class lists

- unit or theme-oriented quotes, posters, or articles
- motivational posters or quotes
- seasonal decorations
- daily announcements, sports schedules, home-room news, and pending school activities
- student contest, competition, or available scholarship applications

Many teachers, especially on the secondary level, share classrooms with other teachers. Talk with the others working in your teaching space. Discuss how bookshelves and file drawers will be shared. Find out which bulletin boards will be yours. If there are no stairs to negotiate and your subject requires a variety of materials and equipment, request a cart or cupboard on wheels. If you will be teaching on several floors, arrange for your own forms, pens, and pencils to be kept in a drawer in each room. Make sure you've left the room as orderly as when you walked in. Is litter off the floor? Is everything you borrowed returned? Are books picked up? Are desks cleaned of any marks? Are boards erased? As petty as it sounds, many hostile relationships have ensued over messy roommates . . . just when you thought your college days were over.

Your Desk   The contents of a teacher's desk are often instrumental in avoiding unnecessary trips from the classroom. Although teachers are no longer able to dispense aspirin, cough drops, or other medication, students, sometimes, have other needs. Safety pins and Band-Aids are often requested. If most teachers had a nickel for all the tissues they donated, they could retire. Tissues are a must! Check to see if tissue is on your supply list. Mary, Kathy, and Marc all add a box of tissue to their students' list of supplies. Even though all students don't bring them, the teachers end up with enough tissue to last the whole year!

A favorite educator who is now a middle school principal was well known for her special

your desk

supplies. As a counselor, she was popular with students, parents, and teachers, not just because she was a bright woman in her field, but also because she was generous and caring. Her office contained everything from thumbtacks to hair spray. She remedied ailments from static cling to shattered egos.

Keeping often-needed items available saves time, eliminates unnecessary trips to the rest-room, and conveys to students that you care about them. Most students won't abuse these freebies.

This is not to suggest that you become the building pharmacist and supplier, however. Especially if you're a beginning teacher, you'll have other financial priorities, and no one expects you to make these purchases. If you do, however, save your receipts, as these may be tax deductible when you file your income taxes. Investigate your school's purchasing system in order to obtain as many supplies as possible. Policies vary among school systems.

When Marc, a math teacher, took his first assignment at a middle school he was fortunate in obtaining an almost unlimited amount of supplies. When he needed a bottle of liquid paper or a new stapler, he simply marched down to the supply room and took what he needed. Eight years later, he transferred to another school, naively expecting the same privileges. Wrong! The first day, when the old-timers were carting off their new boxes of supplies, Marc had none. He hadn't been there the previous spring to order. A few teachers did dig in and provide him with spare pens, and extra rolls of tape, but supply-wise it was a tight year, and a lot of what went into Marc's classroom came from his personal budget.

An inventory of a teacher's desk might include:

- file folders
- stick-on notes or notepads (great for separating papers and brief notes to students)
- cellophane and masking tape with dispensers
- thumbtacks or push pins
- stapler and as many boxes of staples as your budget can afford (start with two)
- triple-size or regular chalk if you have chalk boards; if you have white boards, see if you can order dry-erase markers continuously, as these don't store well and tend to dry out
- paper clips (all sizes)
- several calendars
- rulers
- compass and three-whole punch
- pens, pencils, and erasers
- rubber cement and glue
- felt-tip markers (water-based and permanent)
- scissors
- rubber bands
- staple remover
- extra computer disks
- blank cassettes
- transparency or acetate sheets for overhead projectors and AV pens (blue, black, or brown are easiest for students to see; yellow and orange will probably collect in your drawer)

In one drawer, keep a file containing schedules that have been distributed, memos concerning procedures or important dates, and forms pertaining to students (transfer forms, accident reports, classroom management and tardy forms, and others that are not electronic). Retain this file and update it yearly. It is helpful, for example, to know specialists' schedules.

You may also want to keep some personal items in your desk such as:

- breath mints and a small mirror (If you have parsley on your teeth, most students won't tell you; they will, however, inform most of the student body.)
- thank-you notes
- antibacterial wipes, soap, or lotion (Frequent hand-washing and chalk dust, if you use chalk, dries skin like desert sand.)
- deodorant (for that busy morning when you forget)
- spare nylons and personal hygiene items
- latex gloves (critical when exposed to bodily fluids)

Be aware that any material that isn't cemented down can escape from the classroom. Through the years, Bill, a high school Spanish teacher, has "lost" books, coats, a wallet (with numerous credit cards), disks, pens, his favorite Albert Einstein poster, plants, tape dispensers, scissors, and half-eaten candy bars. Do not bring books that your first lover gave you for Christmas, the orchid that you have been nurturing since 1986, or a poster from Earth Day unless you wish to donate them. Anything of value—and this includes tests and other materials you wish to keep from sticky fingers—should be left at home or locked in a file cabinet. Password protection should limit access to your computer.

Regardless of what professional and personal items you choose to keep at school, your individual style will influence how you organize your workspace. Gary has a desk that would make a drill sergeant smile, while the top of Marc's is usually cluttered with student papers, day-old passes, a plant, and a photo from a summer vacation to

Yellowstone. Buried beneath the chaos is a desk-top calendar, which Marc does manage to check daily. Both Gary and Marc have shelves within their grasp that house reference books, current texts, a dictionary, a thesaurus, and a current copy of *Writers INC.* (a handy little manual which, regardless of your grade level or discipline, is a treasure). They also have curriculum guides, electronic resources, and print materials that aid in lesson planning.

Shared Equipment and Materials   Consider where to keep shared materials such as tape dispensers and staplers. Set up an area for these items on the counter, shelf, or bookcase, and clearly label where each tool is kept. Pictorial symbols as well as labels will help with quick location and replacement of items.

If possible, your room should contain software available at learning centers where students have access to encyclopedias, dictionaries, thesauri, and other material applicable to the curricula you're teaching. CDs will need to be carefully monitored, as these are apt to disappear easily and quickly. Perhaps room sets of encyclopedias and dictionaries can be available for students if it's not possible for all students to be using computers for research. Your inventory should also include crayons, glue, scissors, scratch or construction paper, and old magazines and newspapers so that your lessons will appeal to a variety of learners.

Desks, Windows, and Exits   If you have access to roster printouts prior to opening day, check the number of desks with expected students. Are there enough? Talk with the custodian and respectfully communicate your needs. If your room has windows, check to see if there are shades or blinds to keep the sun from students' eyes and to darken the room for films. Cardboard or posters may work in a pinch. If there are no windows, is there a fan for circulation? Check to see that outlets and lights work properly. Be certain that you've familiarized yourself with emergency exits and the route you and your students will take during fire drills.

Seat Arrangement   The arrangement of student desks or tables influences the classroom environment. When you're setting up your classroom, consider your goals and planned types of activities as you contemplate room arrangement. Traditional rows are still appropriate for some lessons and are sometimes practical, depending on the size of the room. When you want to foster small-group discussion, cooperation, teamwork, or tutoring, arrange the desks in clusters. Ideal group sizes range from two to four students. When students need space for working independently or calming themselves, the desks can be easily moved. Chapter 4 provides more complete information on establishing and managing groups.

Time spent at the beginning of the year teaching students how to move their desks safely and efficiently will save you time and back problems later. Then, when the room needs to be rearranged, a quick sketch on the board or masking tape on the floor lets students know where to move.

Let students know that they have the responsibility to choose the kind of environment in which they would like to work. They should regard your permission to change positions in the room frequently as a privilege. If one or two students are unable to move desks without creating havoc, then they might lose this opportunity.

When planning your room arrangement, you can save time by drawing a simple sketch of your room and planning on paper. Think about traffic flow and the kinds of activities you will be involved in. Use stick-notes to represent desks, tables, or computer stations. You can easily move these around the diagram, yet they'll stay put once you've made your decision.

OPENING DAY

Once your room is transformed into an environment that invites rather than intimidates, and your desk and supplies are in order, you can begin concentrating on the first day. The opening of school bustles with eager as well as fearful faces. Old relationships are reestablished; students and staff anticipate another passage. Elementary, middle, and secondary schools all share the vitality that marks the first day of another school year.

Administrative Duties

Many schools do not meet for a full opening day. In middle and high schools, the first time you meet with your students may vary from ten to thirty minutes. Usually you'll have administrative duties to attend to. The first day might involve:

1. Writing your name and the title of the class on the board or TV monitor. This also encourages students to check for daily assignments, objectives, and activities.
2. Checking students in. This may involve initialing a computer printout or schedule.
3. Creating a seating chart. You may decide to change this later, but it helps you in taking roll and learning students' names.
4. Assessing some information about your students: their hobbies and interests; what they learned last year; what goals they have for this year. You could use student surveys or personal information sheets (see pages 55 and 56) to gather information.

Students' First Impressions of You

It is important to let students know immediately that you are the professional. This means looking, sounding, and acting the part. Until students know from experience that you are competent, fair, consistent, and caring, they will quickly assess you, based on

STUDENT SURVEY

1. Your full name: _____

2. The name you'd like to be called in class

   _____

3. Age: _____   4. Birthday: _____

5. Home phone: _____

6. What school did you attend last year? (Add
   the city and state) _____

7. Who was your English teacher last year?

   _____

8. What is your favorite subject? _____

9. What is your most disliked or worst subject?

   _____

10. What hobbies or activities do you enjoy?

    _____

11. What is something you do well? _____

12. What is your most treasured possession?

    _____

13. If you had an entire day to spend as you
    wished, what would you do? _____

14. If you could change one thing about
    yourself, what would you change?

    _____

15. What do you plan to do after high school?

    _____

16. How many people are in your family? ____

17. Do you have any pets? _____

18. What else would you like me to know
    about you?   _____

PERSONAL INFORMATION SHEET

STUDENT'S NAME _____

PARENTS' NAME(S) _____

ADDRESS_____

HOME   WORK   MOM _____

PHONE _____   PHONE   DAD _____

DOES THE STUDENT WALK TO SCHOOL? ____
RIDE A BUS? ____

BUS # _____

GO TO A SITTER OR CARE CENTER
BEFORE/AFTER SCHOOL? _____

NAME _____

PHONE # OF CAREGIVER _____

PERSON TO CALL IN CASE OF EMERGENCY _____

PHONE _____

SPECIAL NOTES (health problems, food allergies, etc.) ____

_____

_____

_____

_____

---

their first impression. You can convey confidence and a sense of self-pride through dress, voice, and body language.

Dress and Personal Appearance   As discussed in Chapter 1, dress is critical in communicating a message to students. Professional dress helps establish credibility. Even in physical education classes, it is a good idea to "dress up" on nonactivity days. Since many art or science instructors wear smocks, they often wear sport coats or jackets underneath.

If you are a young teacher or just beginning, it is all the more critical that you establish your role as the teacher. Many young women have resorted to different hairstyles to look more authoritative. Tami, an attractive young science teacher, was having problems establishing herself as the teacher; she looked like her students. A friend in her department suggested that she try wearing her blonde mane on top of her head. The transformation really helped. Nick, a band instructor, was complaining of a similar problem: "My students keep telling me how *young* I look," he'd say. "I know it's a compliment, but I think they would respect me more if I didn't appear so close to their own ages." Nick grew a moustache and that, coupled with the other tips he received on effective classroom management, helped.

This doesn't mean that you need to emulate the stereotypical image of the schoolmarm or master of old. It simply suggests that dress and personal appearance are vital to establishing the tone that is so critical when meeting students. It's also important to understand your building principal's stand on dress. To some, it's a major priority; to others, it's not as important.

Voice Control Effective teachers articulate and enunciate. Could you become more effective by speaking louder and practicing voice control? Tape-record your voice and videotape your teaching; evaluate how you sound and look. Invite a colleague to sit in the back of your room and provide feedback about your delivery.

Because students are also cued visually, it's a bonus to be animated. Brian is a favorite with many students because his presence commands their attention. He's animated, vocal, and clear. He moves around the room when he lectures. You won't find students sleeping in Brian's class.

Grammar and Usage Correct grammar and usage are critical. Although many students may not realize the difference between an object pronoun and a subject pronoun, many others will. If you use poor English, your credibility is severely at risk, not just with those students, but with their parents—who will be quick to criticize. Quizzes, tests, progress reports, and other communication should be error-free.

If you squeaked by in college with shaky grammar, either review a text on usage or consult an English teacher in your building. It's done all the time: "Mary, I always get confused; is it correct to say, 'With Jim and me or with Jim and I?'" Not only will you improve your speech, but also the teacher you ask will be glad you did. *Writers INC.* is another excellent source for quick reference. The spell check feature in most word processing programs is designed to alleviate problems. Be accurate. We reflect on each other.

Body Language   Like Brian, effective teachers use body language. Move among your students. During group work pull up a chair and talk with them. Check for understanding and that students are on task as you move around the room. Proximity reduces discipline problems. No one likes to listen to someone drone on as he or she stands firmly behind a podium. Most teachers agree that they're performers. Some view themselves as salespeople with a product to "sell."

Opening Assignment

Once you've established your expectations, it's important to create an atmosphere that is comfortable and nonthreatening, yet academic and businesslike. Many teachers begin the year with some sort of survey or information sheet that asks about students' hobbies and interests. Mary, a secondary reading teacher, uses this technique; while her students are working, Mary moves between the aisles or among tables, noting students' names and what they wish to be called in class.

Learning Students' Names

Learning students' names quickly enables you to deal with discipline problems immediately. Mike, a kindergarten teacher, shares a vivid memory of a first day of school when he was reading *Miss Eva and the Red Balloon* to his students. Mike was entertaining them with his most expressive voice, and making eye contact as 24 five- and six-year olds listened with rapt attention. Mike noticed one young man not paying attention to the story; fortunately he had learned the student's name. Mike firmly stated the child's name and placed the boy within arm's reach, solving the problem. Mike continued his dramatic reading and the atmosphere remained intact. Mike is skilled at putting names and faces together quickly. If you have a more difficult time, you can employ a variety of techniques and mnemonic devices to learn your students' names: Name tags, desk tags, and seating charts are a few. If your students do not have assigned seating or move around frequently, the students may have to wear name tags until you and they become acquainted. Saying the student's name while looking at him or her is effective. One resourceful teacher won the name game for himself and his substitute when, on the first day, he grouped three or four students together and snapped their picture. He developed the film, cut apart the pictures, and glued the pictures on a file folder in the same configuration as the seats. He labeled each photo with the student's name. The teacher kept the folder on his podium so he could refer to it. He can move or rearrange the photos as the need arises.

While students are working, look at your name list and make mental notes. Try associating some feature with the name. This may sound silly, but it works. If Tim has red hair and freckles, think of an association that will help you remember: a red-haired Tiny Tim on crutches, perhaps. A social studies teacher gave an example of a boy in class named Scott. She mentally placed a tartan cap on his head. Whatever it takes, the sooner you learn students' names, the better.

THE FIRST WEEK—STUDY TEAMS

The first week of school is usually hectic. Even in the most "settled" of schools, some students will be trickling in all week. Electronic grade books, fortunately, can be edited quickly.

Establishing study teams is one method of getting acquainted with the class and conveying the idea that the responsibility for learning rests with the students, as well as with the teacher. When a student is absent, other study team members may collect notes, assignments, or handouts for that absent study team member. Marc suggests establishing study teams in the following way: Assign three or four members to each group. Attempt to make your group as heterogeneous as possible. Choose members with different abilities, interests, and counselors. One purpose of the team is to assist absent students. It's important that all group members are not in the same activities. Band members frequently miss the same days, for example. Because you don't know your students well yet, you may base your decisions on where they sit. Students who know each other usually choose to sit together. Assign groups from varying parts of the room.

The first group activity might be to answer several questions on the board, overhead, or handout.

- What is your name?
- What are your hobbies?
- What is your favorite movie/song/book?
- Who is your favorite person?
- When is your birthday?
- What do you think we'll be studying in class this year?

Tell the students to write the questions down and meet for fifteen to twenty minutes in their groups. During that time, the students are to interview each other. Inform them that they will, ultimately, be introducing their group members to the rest of the class. These ice-breaking questions engage groups in dialogues that will introduce them to each other. Circulate among the groups, encouraging shyer students.

When the discussion time has elapsed, bring the groups back together. Inform them that they are going to make a group collage. The collage must reflect words, phrases, and pictures that represent the groups' interests as well as the individuals'. Explain that, by the end of the hour the next day, the group will introduce each other, using the collage as a visual aid. The collages will be hung in the room. Supply the group with old newspapers and magazines, scissors, glue, and construction paper.

This activity not only provides the students with a team, it also provides you some valuable insight about your students.

NEW STUDENTS

At the beginning of the year, you will often need to admit a new student. In the middle of a class discussion, a new face will appear at the door, and the student will hand you a sign-in slip. The new student is probably more embarrassed and frustrated about interrupting your class than you can imagine. Smile, then take a moment to whisper quickly that the student may take a seat and you'll be with him or her in a moment. If possible, a vacant chair or desk near the door is excellent for these new students. Your file containing introductory handouts should be handy; you can give these to the new student to peruse until you can give the student your attention. Assign him or her a study team, text, and book, and take a moment to find out where the student came from and what was being studied in the last school. Generally, a student has been uprooted because of family changes. Many are upset about the shift. A few kind words of welcome will help the student believe that there might be a bright spot in the transfer.

CONCLUSION

Overall, the primary message in this chapter is to be prepared. Know your building and make sure you're organized in both your classroom and expectations. As in building a house, the structure is as strong or as shaky as its foundation.

chapter four

Curriculum: Design Strategies

> ① My advice for a new teacher would be to take a deep breath and relax. We are children, not aliens. Treat us with respect and & asert authority. Be creative, not cautzious. Let your imagination teach us, not a text book.
>
> *Laurel Talley*

Enthusiasm, anchored in background knowledge, is vitally important in teaching because expertise and your passion for educating students contribute immensely to student motivation. The effective teacher recognizes the varying abilities of students within a class. This teacher also knows that students learn in different ways; the task is to accommodate those differences while challenging students to develop their maximum potentials.

IF THERE IS A SCOPE AND SEQUENCE AND/OR DISTRICT CURRICULUM

Your district's published scope and sequence or curriculum guide dictates what to teach. The advantage of a school district's having a curriculum is that you will know exactly what units to cover during the year. Although this is the ideal theory, it is not the reality. No matter what content is offered to students and no matter in what order, not all students arrive in class ready to learn the material. Some transfer in from other schools, some were ill the week the preparatory skill was introduced, some are dealing with emotional problems, some are not developmentally ready, and some simply didn't care enough to learn.

Sometimes teachers are to blame for voids in the curriculum. Instead of adhering to the scope and sequence, they teach their "specialties" or digress from the curriculum simply because they do not like being told what to teach. Others have difficulty meeting the requirements due to lack of books, support materials, lab equipment, or specific physical facilities. Occasionally, teachers encounter difficulties when they religiously stick to the curriculum, ignoring the personalities and individual abilities of their charges.

You must strive to reach a balance between the established scope and sequence, individual student differences, and your personal style. Find out if a curriculum for the assigned class exists and (sometimes the hard part) obtain one. Ask your department chair, principal, or curriculum coordinator for a copy. Regardless of the age, quality, or completeness of curriculum, it can provide a path of continuity, especially during those first teaching years when you must be concerned with so many bewildering details. You are accountable for teaching the contents of the curriculum, not the text. The text supports the goals, objectives, and skills outlined in the curriculum guide.

Administrative Expectations

Find out what your administrator expects. Are the teachers in your department required to be at a certain point at the end of each grading period? Does the administrator evaluate your use of the curriculum as part of your performance? Most often, administrators are concerned with classroom management and lesson design.

COMPETENCY TESTS

Know if the students are required to take a subject competency test or state regent's test at the end of the year. As the various tests approach, lessons in how to take tests, how to manage time, and how to correctly interpret directions are appropriate. Test jitters can be alleviated or controlled when students know what to expect and what to do during the administration of a standardized test.

Intent of Curriculum

Skim through the curriculum. Is it written as a day-by-day plan or is it a collection of possible lessons to teach within a unit? You are not expected to teach every lesson included. Pick and choose those that will work for you and implement your own creative ideas for lessons that will teach or reinforce the skills and concepts.

Materials for Each Unit

Read through the first several units carefully. Are the necessary books, teaching materials, and space for activities available? Look several units ahead to prevent surprises. Ask where the materials are kept: Are they kept within the building or are they at a resource center in the district? Another teacher, the principal, the head secretary, or the custodian may know the answers. Determine if the needed materials can be ordered and arrive in time for your use in teaching the lesson. It's often true that if ordered material is promised for Monday, it may not arrive until Wednesday. If needed material isn't available, design an original lesson or consult with an experienced teacher about how to teach that concept.

Integrating the Curriculum

When you are teaching elementary school, it is often appropriate to integrate subject matter. After you have previewed different curriculum guides and texts, you may notice that in spelling, reading, and language the skill of recognizing homophones is introduced. Consider integrating different parts of the curriculum on this concept. Use the stories, wordlists, worksheets, and other extending activities from all subject areas during the unit.

Another time to integrate the curriculum might be when you teach the skills of comparing, measuring, and estimating. These concepts are commonly covered in math and science texts. Look through both curricula and texts to determine the activities, vocabulary, and exercises that best support teaching these concepts. You can also find poems or stories that support the concepts of measuring or estimating. Ideally, an elementary curriculum would be totally integrated. You may be fortunate enough to have curriculum guides that cross-reference subject areas; if not, look for connections. Notes and reflections from your lesson plans will serve as a starting point when you begin planning more integrated lessons for the following year. Reinforce what you are studying by using vocabulary in written assignments and making references to this material when working in other subject areas.

IF THERE IS NO CURRICULUM

Quality curriculum development is the mixture of a needs assessment, effective strategies, teaching experience, background knowledge, and curriculum writing techniques. Quality curriculum develops when there is time for discussion and contemplation; this seldom occurs in the whirlwind of the school year—even for experienced teachers.

If you are assigned to teach a semester or yearlong course for which no curriculum exists, here are some specific guidelines for survival:

1. Consult a colleague teaching the same class and ask what he or she covers and in what order. If no one else teaches that course, consult the teacher's guide for the assigned text. Teacher's editions usually contain scope and sequence charts for your grade level. Use these charts as models. If no guide exists, use the table of contents as a possible overview for the class.
2. Keep in mind the grade level being taught, student needs, and the sociological profile of the community. A town in which everyone works at the same industrial factory or a small farming community will likely require a different approach to curriculum than a large urban community.
3. Keep your expectations high and challenge your students creatively and intellectually.

Arrangement of Curriculum

History and literature courses are usually arranged chronologically or thematically. Math, writing, art, and physical education classes are developmentally taught, where new skills are based on previous learning. Sciences, including lab sciences, are usually taught systemically or by concept.

The first unit you choose to teach can go a long way in setting the tone and proving your credibility.

The unit should showcase the teaching techniques with which you are most comfortable. This unit also needs to be tightly structured, organized, and challenging. Robert begins the year with an integrated unit based on Robert McCloskey's stories. He assesses students' knowledge of word families with activities from *Make Way for Ducklings*. He invents math problems about counting donuts using *Homer Price*. The loss of a first tooth in *One Morning in Maine* initiates a writing activity about his students' own "firsts." Betty, a high school language arts teacher, saves a unit on satire and humor for the last three weeks of school. The tasks seem easier and her juniors are more relaxed: They end the class on a high note.

Plan for logical divisions between units that coincide with vacations and grading periods. Carrying a unit over a grading period or a vacation can be frustrating for both you and your students. Rearrange sections so that you finish an assignment just before the vacation or grading period. When students return to their work, a short review of the prior lesson can provide the beginning focus for the next concept in that unit. You might teach a short novel between Thanksgiving and the winter holidays, completing the reading and analysis writing several days before vacation. Students then could use those last, restless days to finish projects or to present skits based on the novel. Save that long, tough series of lessons on cell division or genetics for after vacation.

Connect the previous unit to the new one. Students comprehend better when they see relationships to previous learning. Students often create original links of their own between concepts. A teacher needs to be open to allowing all students to develop and express their own connections. What might be obvious to you might not be to them. Find ways to help them make the transition. When Betty finishes her unit on Emerson and Thoreau, she has students list all the beliefs of the transcendentalists. Student groups identify modern examples for many of these characteristics, and posters show the connections they made. Then Betty uses a different color marker to write the opposites and introduces Herman Melville and the antitranscendentalists.

When preparing a series of daily lessons, plan more work than you can expect to finish. This way, if the students know more than you anticipated or worked more quickly than you estimated, they will still have a full period of practice and reinforcement. If the technology you planned to use failed or the video you ordered didn't arrive, you will have other activities to substitute.

If you plan a lesson and the students finish early, have alternate activities ready. *Slack time breeds classroom management problems.* Few will quietly pick up a library book or review old math problems. Fewer still will sit quietly and allow slower students a chance to catch up. Elementary students are more likely to enjoy puzzles, games, related reading, or activity centers for enrichment during these slack times. The best strategy is to plan for more than the entire period and drop some of the activities as time draws to an end. Having extra activities planned that pertain to a unit allows you to add them when you have extra time or when a lesson plan goes awry.

Duplicated Materials

You will need multiple copies when each child needs access to a copied page or worksheet. Find out about the policy on duplicating. The school might require a forty-eight-hour turnover time for duplication services. Other schools have facilities for self-service. Plan ahead because copy machines frequently need service, making them temporarily unavailable, or there will be others in line to copy before you.

Be aware of the legal limitations of copyright law. Your media specialist should be the most knowledgeable about the recent changes regarding copying materials from printed or electronic sources. Many books state that you may copy pages for classroom use. When you do the copying, show the source at the bottom of the page. When you use a worksheet authored by a colleague, give that colleague credit as the source.

Evaluation Methods

As you develop the unit, plan your methods of evaluation. If you give objective tests, jot down possible questions with each objective. Note questions that students ask in class. Think about subjective methods of evaluating what students learn. Think about methods of evaluating the various activities you plan for the unit. See the section on test writing later in this chapter.

PLANNING LESSONS THAT UTILIZE GROUPS

As the workplace is changing, so is the need for collaborative skills. Businesses from banking to food service indicate the need for individuals who can get along well with others. Curriculum activities utilizing cooperative groups teach both the subject objectives and the social skills necessary for success in the world of work. All group activities should move toward specific goals. A variety of well-planned exercises may result in a noisy classroom, but this doesn't mean students aren't learning. Noisy students are usually involved and enthusiastic. Regardless of age level or subject area, group work can set up situations in which students are challenged to use higher levels of thinking and develop social skills.

Start with a few well-planned, short, group activities until you and your students feel comfortable with the process. Students need specific guidelines for acceptable behavior, the group task, individual roles, time to complete the task, and evaluation.

Creating Groups

As you plan group activities, organize lessons that teach or reinforce social skills. While we work toward making them second nature, listening, expressing opinions, and sharing materials are not innate. When you form groups, consider your goals. Your goal may dictate a heterogeneous group balancing student abilities, genders, learning styles, and personality types. The goal may be best met by grouping students with similar skill levels or interests. Random grouping can be done by counting off: For example, twenty-eight students can count off in sevens to form groups of

Group Work

four. You might put colored cards on desks before class and ask students to group by colors. Occasionally, have students choose their own groups. The privilege of selecting their own group gives added responsibility to the students. Ideal group size ranges from two to four students.

After students are grouped, think about necessary social skills. You could plan a brainstorming session for the first group activity. Have each group discuss a social skill and describe what it would look and sound like as everyone is practicing that skill. Model the kinds of responses you expect the groups to produce. If group one is focusing on providing encouragement, you might hear students saying, "That is a good point," or, "Jane, I like what you just said." Desks will be in clusters, and you will see people looking at each other and leaning forward as they talk.

Your role during group activities is moving around the room, meeting with the groups periodically, checking to make sure the students are on task, observing the students as they work, and answering questions. Watch for individuals who dominate the group or withdraw. Assigning roles helps eliminate problems. Question those who don't appear to be contributing. Offer encouragement to build self-confidence. Do not dominate the group yourself. Offer suggestions if students seem to be laboring too long over an issue. Often a casual suggestion is all it takes to start the ball rolling. After the group has finished a task, have them evaluate how well they worked as a group. This group processing will improve the group's functions on its next task.

Keys to Group Success

■ Tell the group how long they have to complete the task and write the time on the board, overhead, or on the TV monitor. Assign one student as the timekeeper. As you move around the room, consult with the timekeeper. This helps keep students on task.

- Assign one person as the scribe or secretary; this person's task is to take notes on group discussion.
- Assign one person as the reporter, whose job is to paraphrase or read the information to the class.
- Assign one person as the resource person; this individual's job is to gather the needed material, make sure the assignment is turned in, and make sure the group cleans its workspace at the end of the project. This is the person who can come to you with a question after the group has exhausted its personal resources to find an answer. By limiting who can ask you questions, you force group members to consult each other.
- Rotate assignments with each group session so all students practice all roles.

There are some alternatives to small-group work. Jigsaw style activities begin using small groups and end up working as large groups. This pattern is effective when reviewing.

LEARNING STYLES

Knowledge about learning styles helps you better plan lessons and appeal to a variety of learners so that more of your students—not just those who respond to your teaching style—learn the concepts. Exposing students to how they learn gives them control of their own learning plus a better understanding of those who assimilate differently.

Following are a few tips for planning lessons to accommodate the variety of learning styles you will find in your classroom:

- Some students need to sit in the front of the room so they can concentrate and not be distracted by others. Some students need to sit in the back so they'll feel safe when they see other students working on the same tasks.

- Tactile learners need to use manipulatives to help them learn and remember. They need to count objects and learn by moving things around. These youngsters will take volumes of notes, chew pencils, hair, or jewelry, scribble in margins, or draw.
- Kinesthetic learners use their whole bodies to learn. Elementary children might trace the letters of the alphabet using a whole arm. They might form each letter with arms and legs. These students love performing skits or telling original stories by roaming around the room, picking up appropriate props when needed.
- Restless learners need lots of movement. This movement may take the form of stray trips to the pencil sharpener, wastebasket, or computer center. Be tolerant of this movement, but at the same time, teach students that there are inappropriate times to move about: during a lecture, student presentation, video, or assignment directions. On days you know the students will be restless (homecoming, Halloween, assemblies, the days before vacations), plan movement even if it involves just moving in and out of small groups. You might schedule a thirty-second stretch at intervals.

- Continual talkers are not to be confused with students who chatter socially when they should be focused on class work. Those who are learning by talking continually are those who mutter to themselves as they write or work on math problems. These learners need to see it, say it, and hear it to learn new material. Surround these students with others who do not mind background noise while they are doing their own work.
- Some students are affected by the time of day. One reason students fail at day school is that they are at their best in the evening and might be more successful in night school. Some coping techniques for these kinds of students include their taking more notes in the most frustrating classes, completing homework and test review during optimum learning times, studying in half-hour segments during their less focused times, and making appointments with the teacher for short review sessions before a test.
- Room temperature will affect some students and not others. Move students who prefer warmth away from windows, doors, and fans. Encourage students to dress appropriately for their individual preferences. Inform students if there is very little control over the climate of your room. They have more control by altering their dress.
- Some students learn better when they eat as they work. You may agree with the concept in theory, but still not want students eating or drinking in your classroom. You might find it distracting and, inevitably, you will end up with half-filled soda cans, wrappers, and abandoned gum. Your school may or may not have a rule about eating in the classroom. If not, your personal desires prevail. Another consideration is that medical research encourages water consumption, but that brings increased restroom trips.

- Your room arrangement can reflect your teaching style as well as your students' learning styles. Sometimes the subject matter or activity plan might dictate the arrangement. Keep in mind that walking into a rearranged room will distress some students. If you want to startle students and capture their attention with the novelty, don't tell them before you rearrange. If you don't want them distracted by the new configuration, warn them the day before. Students might choose how they would like the room arranged as long as they don't insist that your desk be in the hall.
- Some students learn better auditorily, others visually. When Betty was a fifth grader, she had a teacher who would give a daily oral math problem $(3 + 2 \times 7 - 4)$. The student who got the answer first went to lunch first that day. Betty never went to lunch first that year, but she did get the message that she was not proficient in math. In high school, Betty could never figure out why she scored so high on the math sections of standardized tests. Now she knows she is capable in math, but she is not an auditory learner. She needs to repeat aloud, take notes, or read along as she listens.

As a teacher, you can write important points on the board, an overhead, or computer connected to the TV monitor as you speak. You can use these same tools to emphasize oral directions or write out math problems. The same information can be handed to more visual learners on paper so they can read along and take additional notes as you speak.

Other students remember everything they hear, but have problems comprehending what they read. These students need to take notes as they read, underline phrases in books they own, or keep journal entries summarizing short sections of their reading assignments. These same students will ask you what you mean by a certain question on a test. All you need to do is read the question aloud without explanation and they will usually say, "Oh, yeah, I get it now." Read test directions aloud as students read them silently and explain that this technique supports both auditory and visual learners.

- Learning style researchers study brain preference or brain dominance that is reflected in global or analytic tendencies. Here's a quick inventory to do with students to identify if they tend to learn analytically or globally:

"I'm going to describe two approaches to the same situation. When I finish, I'm going to ask which approach is more like you.

"When we are hiking in Yellowstone, my husband will suddenly point and say, 'Look at that owl in the tree.' I look in that direction and see the forest, the sky, and the meadow in front. Then, slowly, I will be able to pick out the brown bird deep in the branches of a nearby tree. My husband sees the owl first. Then he notices the trees, the sky, and the meadow.

"Now, what kind of learner are you? Do you see the forest first, then the details? Or do you see the detail first and then notice everything else?"

Those "forest-seers" are global learners and like overviews and large concepts. Those "detail folks" are more analytic and want the facts in the proper order—not the big picture. Emphasize that both are equally acceptable approaches to learning; then structure lessons with components that appeal to both kinds of learners. When giving directions, talk about the whole project and what the end product will look like and then outline the steps necessary to complete the task.

- Some students work and learn best in groups while others abhor these experiences and become stressed. Allow students to choose to work by themselves on some assignments unless the objective of the assignment is to improve group skills. If group participation is a component of the lessons and can't be avoided, make the next assignment an "alone" project to provide balance. This balance can be applied to student responses. To give variety to your classes and allow students with different talents to shine, include choices to write, present orally, or illustrate. These response choices need to reflect the learning objective and be choices that you find equivalent, acceptable, and gradeable.

■ In the course of a unit or lesson, every major learning style should be utilized. You will then appeal to the learning strength of every student in your class. Provide students with a variety of stimuli to help them learn the new material. Present the material orally and visually. Plan practice activities for students that appeal to their different learning styles. Offer a variety of ways for students to demonstrate what they have learned. In addition, offer extension activities that help students both move beyond the new knowledge and connect that material meaningfully with their own world.

VARIETY IN THE DAY'S LESSON

We hope, as you read through this book, you notice that we try to offer a variety of ideas to appeal to all types of learners and teachers. Rule Number 1 in choosing teaching ideas is that if you feel awkward or uncomfortable doing an activity that has worked for someone else, don't do it. Use what you are comfortable with and include a variety of strategies whenever possible. Here are some more ideas:

■ Start with a short activity to focus the lesson. This activity should engage every student. It could be a five-point quiz, a cartoon or phrase on the board to be discussed, an open-ended question for a journal response, or a brainstorm session gathering current knowledge on a topic. As soon as you finish taking roll, walk around the room, recording points for completion of this first task and asking different students to write parts of their responses on the board. This keeps students accountable and gives you a starting point for the day's work. Brian frequently walks into his government class, newspaper in hand, and asks, "How many of you read the story this morning about . . . ?" Soon a majority of the students are skimming the newspaper before arriving in class.

▪ After stimulating interest, present the day's lesson. This might involve note taking, so include tips to help students improve these skills as they take notes on content material. Model what you expect in their notes by writing on the board, the overhead, or the computer/TV monitor setup. Giving slower students a partial outline of the material will help them see your organization and help them listen better for missing points. Within this same class period, students might review this new material by completing group activities using their notes. Groups might be asked to summarize the material from a different point of view. History students could respond to "What would General Patton say about the Gulf War?" Language arts students could express what they know about transcendentalism by discussing how Emerson would evaluate contemporary American philosophies. Elementary students could tell what it would have been like for the astronauts to meet the Pilgrims. This rearranging of the day's new material is a great time to help students make connections in their own lives. Use the last minutes of class to have students review what they learned that day, tell you what their next assignment is, and make one new connection with the day's concepts.

■ Subsequent lessons might involve a day in the media center researching or a day in the computer lab searching for related topics. Results could be shared through posters, presentation software, or oral reports by individuals or groups. At the end of the unit, after graded evaluations, provide the students with extension activities such as a chance to perform skits based on the unit or a field trip. Within each unit and within each day, try to plan for something to strain the brain, something to smile over, an excuse to move around, and a reason for a student to talk to another about school. Plan an exacting assignment for your analytical students and a more multitasked assignment to appeal to your global students. Try to vary activities at twenty-minute intervals.

One thing we never have enough of in our lessons is *think time.* "Take two minutes to think quietly about the bizarre relationships among the characters in 'The Fall of the House of Usher.'" After these two minutes, students may record their thoughts in journals. These thoughts could provide a focus activity for the next day's lesson. Teachers often get so busy occupying every minute of class that students do not get time to process what they are learning. Of course, there's a Catch-22 to "think time": Is the student really thinking about Roderick Usher's relationship with Madeline, or musing on last week's dance? Making the student accountable (jotting ideas in a journal or sharing with the class) usually keeps each on task.

THOUGHTS ON JOURNALS

The use of student journals, while widespread, is often a perplexing topic. Student journals/logs can range from a few pages stapled together, to spiral notebooks of varying sizes, to clothbound blank books purchased at a bookstore. The following suggestions are made for using this learning tool.

- The journal of a kindergarten student might be a wallpaper-covered book with pages that the student fills with symbolic representations of thoughts and feelings. They include pictures of houses or family members, or drawings of classroom plants in various stages of growth and development.
- As children become more competent readers and writers, the symbols begin to take on the conventions of writing. Primary students use their journals to respond to daily occurrences in and out of the classroom. If students have just returned from a field trip, the teacher might ask them to write and draw their observations. The next day the journal may be used to respond to a different topic or question. The teacher may write comments in each child's journal or direct students to exchange with classmates for reading and responding.

From elementary grades through high school, students begin using separate journals for different subjects. These notebooks may be called thinking, reading, or observation logs, and they are instrumental in developing critical thinking skills and writing fluency in all subject areas.

- Logs can be used at the beginning, middle, or end of a class period to record the lesson objective, the assignment and due date, or a response to a prompt. Writing serves to focus students. These journals can be shared with other students or collected by the teacher. Students can earn a completion grade or points for this writing. Asking students to write a summary-response to the day's lesson allows them to collect and review their thoughts about the material.

- Logs might be used during the lesson for note taking, problem solving, idea summarizing, or reflecting on a concept. Ideas may be generated for essays, poems, tests, or future assignments. Students predict an outcome of a science experiment or what will happen in the next chapter. These logs allow students a chance to think and respond at their various learning levels.

- Collecting journals at intervals holds students accountable and dignifies each individual's thoughts. No matter how a journal is used, teachers must always respect student privacy. No journal entry should be shared with anyone without a student's permission. However, when teachers first introduce journal writing to the class, they must also explain that instructors are bound by law to report illegal occurrences or life-threatening situations.

PLANNING LESSONS

Studies suggest that the experienced and novice teacher spend about the same amount of time planning lessons, but experienced teachers do a great deal of that planning in their heads and write little, while the novice writes volumes. Teaching from either type of lesson plan can be effective, so don't let the sparse or voluminous lesson plan books of colleagues intimidate you. Find out what works for you.

Most schools provide some sort of lesson plan book for the teacher. You might decide that the space is inadequate and instead use tool software such as a spreadsheet program, a spiral notebook, or looseleaf binder to keep track of your daily plans. Save this work for the next year. Your old lesson plans will save you hours of planning time plus providing a pacing guide through the year's units.

Write lesson plans in pencil. Don't consider any plan cast in stone or you will drive yourself crazy long before your retirement party. Be willing to change plans based on student needs, your instincts about the learning process, and outside distractions.

Here's a step-by-step approach that can help you plan lessons:

1. Think over the whole unit and estimate how many days the unit will take. Pencil this information into your lesson plans.
2. Think about major assignments within the unit and the evaluation at the end. How many different assignments will you give? Will the culminating activity be a test, an essay, or a group project? What will be graded?
3. Next, consider how to first capture students' attention and focus it on the topic and how to get students to become aware of what they already know about the topic.
4. Finally, decide what you are going to do day by day, writing your decisions in pencil. Try to formulate fairly comprehensive plans a week in advance. If you work closely with special services teachers, you can send them an overview of your upcoming units so they can help their special needs students in your class meet their deadlines. Music and physical education specialists often like to plan their activities to reflect classroom topics. Media specialists often select lessons, software, and books to complement what is happening in the classroom.

By Wednesday, there will probably be arrows in your plan book, indicating a part of a lesson that got moved to another day because of time restrictions or because students were not ready for that activity. Just because you have the week planned doesn't mean things will always go that way.

When you are writing lesson plans, write what you expect your students to be able to do at the top of each lesson. This will keep you focused on the task of working through the unit's concepts in a logical order. On the day you teach that lesson, tell students the learning goal at the beginning of the session.

Your lesson plan might include the specific dialogue and details you want to cover in your introduction. If you think about all the things you want to say, then actually write them down, you need only to refer to your notes for quick cues and your introduction will appear rehearsed and polished, thus adding to your credibility. Many teachers write out lists of possible questions to help lead discussions. Using Bloom's taxonomy or another schema showing levels of cognitive thinking from recall to evaluation, write out three or more questions on the material at each thinking level. Even if you don't use every one, those questions in your lesson plans can be invaluable in making sure the discussion covers all the concepts in your learning objective. Address all levels of questions to all students. Use these planned questions adroitly and, as the discussion progresses, encourage students to formulate and answer their own questions.

Creative Assignments—Beyond the Text

Many new textbooks include sections listing creative responses for the units or chapters. Skits, science experiments, genre changes, art projects, interviews, computer simulations, presentations via tool software, and role-playing are just some of the many methods that express learning and offer alternatives to traditional assignments. These creative, enrichment assignments often help students relate the material to their own lives, and that increases retention.

You may feel safer avoiding assignments that are loud, messy, or less structured. You should not execute an assignment just because "all the other teachers are doing it," but you will need to choose a variety of activities to accommodate learning differences.

Less traditional activities can be highly rewarding for you and your students. Start by doing one creative project in conjunction with a unit you feel comfortable teaching. If a colleague has used a similar assignment, you might borrow a copy of the directions and ask questions about evaluation. This person can also give you hints about involving students in the evaluation process. The reverse is also true. Do not feel you have to invent a "glitzy" lesson every day. Some days the traditional techniques are the most appropriate.

A creative language arts assignment might follow a study of the stories of Edgar Allan Poe, always a student favorite. Talk to students about "voice" in writing: What word choice and word patterns make a story obviously Poe's? This is a difficult concept for students. When they do understand, they will be able to demonstrate it by rewriting a familiar fairy tale in the voice of Poe. Students will be eager to hear the results, so you might invest a whole class period reading the restructured tales. At the same time, create a situation where every student must actively listen as each tale is read aloud. Designated readers are acceptable. The student can ask the teacher or a friend to read if he or she does not want to. The results are most interesting as the writer coaches the friend or glows with pride. Remaining students list the writer's name on a score sheet (see page 86) and then award one to five points in various categories. Students then tally each score, circling any score over twenty. Students turn in these score sheets and class choices receive special recognition from peers. Your score (frequently close to the class average) determines the grade.

The same student scoring procedure could be used for a social studies assignment to write a poem reflecting the feelings of women or children in wartime. In science, such a class evaluation could be applied to skits about a scientist's life or speculation about the role of science in the future.

Fairy Tales "à la Poe"

Name	Poe-like Vocabu-lary	Interest	Similarity to Original Tale	Original-ity	Poe-like Tone, Feeling	Total

You need only make the score sheet, model a possible response to help students understand how to use the score sheet, and decide what categories will be marked. This scoring system, with criteria changed to suit the assignment, can hold students accountable during student presentations.

Interpretive Posters   These creative approaches to assignments can help students understand and make personal meaning out of a difficult concept. American history students often struggle with the colloquial language of the Declaration of Independence. Students first work in small groups, each working through a short section of the document with the directions to rephrase it into modern language with contemporary examples. Modeling this work might involve a whole-class discussion about who would make a modern substitute for King George. Each group would write out its interpretation and those would be pasted together so that the modernized document could be read as a whole. Students enjoy reading the interpretations from other classes, too. The next step is for each student to choose one sentence or phrase from the document that has personal meaning. Hand each student a sheet of drawing paper and haul out scissors, glue, crayons, and a box of discarded magazines. Each student letters the chosen phrase on the paper and interprets feelings in a magazine-clip-art poster. These are hung in your classroom and could be the basis for a discussion on human rights. Grades on these posters are based on completing the poster on time, following directions, and interpreting the chosen phrase.

AWARDS

Creative projects lend themselves beyond teacher evaluation to student evaluation. Students enjoy seeing and commenting on each other's work while voting for class favorites. Recognition awards need not be elaborate. They can be created out of construction paper and foil, purchased from an art supply store, or produced on your computer. You will see these awards still carefully preserved in desks, lockers, or writing folders at the end of the year. Students may create these awards for each other or themselves. Robert designs a bulletin board for students. Each student has a square of space where he or she is expected to keep a favorite piece of work, memorabilia from a trip, or picture. Many times during the year Robert instructs each student to select a piece of writing or art from his or her portfolio. Students then design awards for one another to display beside this work. The awards reflect one positive aspect of the work.

BORROWING FROM OTHER TEACHERS

Using other teachers' lesson plans, project ideas, and worksheets can be a time-saver. Giving credit to the originator pleases that person, who will then be more likely to share other ideas with you. Writing the author's name on any reproduced material acknowledges copyright. Use these materials judiciously. Borrowed items must suit your content objectives, your teaching needs, and your teaching style. You'll usually borrow a basic idea and modify it. Write the name of the source person on any notes that you keep in your files. This way, if you want more background information about the assignment, you know whom to consult.

Borrowing also implies giving something back. Keep ideas that work successfully tucked away in your mind to share. Experienced teachers do not know it all and welcome fresh ideas to add spark to traditional topics. Some departments or

Sharing Lesson Plans

grade levels hold meetings to share ideas. Everyone leaves feeling rejuvenated with several fresh approaches to tempt their students. If no such group exists, start one on a small scale in your building or through e-mail.

Sharon recently found a suggestion on an electronic bulletin board that she plans to share in the fall with her faculty. The suggestion involves helping a class get to know their teacher. The teacher is to select three to four items (picture, book, or momento) and place them in a paper sack. Each small group of students gets a different sack. The students are to examine the artifacts and use them to create a description of their instructor.

SUBSTITUTE TEACHER FOLDERS

Every teacher should maintain a substitute teacher folder and keep it in a prominent place. These folders are to be used for emergencies when you didn't plan to miss school and had no way of providing

---

A NOTE FROM THE SUB

TODAY WE WERE ABLE TO ACCOMPLISH _____

_____

_____

I THOUGHT THESE THINGS WENT WELL _____

_____

I THOUGHT THE PLANS WERE _____

_____

THESE THINGS NEED YOUR ATTENTION _____

_____

COMMENTS _____

_____

SIGNED _____

Substitute Teacher

Class Summary

Name _____

Date _____

Return to Office at End of Day

Class Period	Absences	Tardies	Cooperative Students

1. Place all papers, assignments, and notices in the regular teacher's mailbox.
2. Sign the "Claim for Substitute" form in the main office *before leaving the building.*

that day's assignment. Some districts produce notebooks or folders specifically for substitutes. Most schools print a two-pocket folder for general use with the school rules and procedures, a spot for a schedule, and a few advertisements printed on it. This makes an ideal sub folder. Add a bright label on the front with the designation "SUB FOLDER," your name, and your room number.

Include a map of the school, an evacuation map, your class or daily schedule, a list of students who attend special classes, your classroom rules, discipline referral forms, a notation about the hall pass policy, the location of your school

Lesson Plans Adequate _____
Lesson Plans Inadequate _____
Substitute Folder Complete _____
Substitute Folder Incomplete _____

Uncooperative Students	Lesson Plan carried out as follows	Specific comments and/or suggestions

3. Please return to main office at the end of the day. Thank you for your cooperation.

policy manual, and current seating charts. (Whenever you change your seating chart, make a practice of putting a copy in your sub folder.) Include a note that will help the substitute teacher detail what happened in class that day. Also include the names of neighboring teachers and the location of restrooms, the vice-principal's office, and the cafeteria.

This folder should also contain a one- or two-day lesson created from material that is relevant to your subject or grade with instructions for presentation. A several-page article or newsletter on a science topic in the news that semester could be

---

SUBSTITUTE TEACHER RESOURCE NOTE

Welcome to our classroom. I appreciate having you fill in for me while I am gone, and I hope this information will help you.

If you have any questions, don't hesitate to ask our principal, _____, or the secretary _____ in room _____ would also be happy to help.

YOU WILL FIND:

LESSON PLANS _____

SUBSTITUTE FOLDER _____

CLASS SCHEDULE _____

SEATING CHART _____

DISCIPLINE PLAN _____

TEACHER'S MANUALS _____

EMERGENCY EVACUATION ROUTE _____

ANY SPECIAL INTRUCTIONS _____

_____

Thank you again for your help.

_____

Classroom teacher

---

the basis for the assignment. Students would form groups to read the article aloud to each other, discuss the material, and complete tasks detailed on the instruction sheet. The sub need only to announce that your absence was an emergency and that he or she will be presenting a short unit relating to the material they have been studying with their teacher. Plan for one or more ways the sub can hold the students accountable: Collect written group responses for a grade, have individual students write and hand in summaries of the article, or give a five-point quiz on the article at the end of the period. The accountability process helps your substitute manage the class effectively. When you do return, acknowledge good behavior and act quickly to address problems. Update this emergency lesson once each grading period.

CREATING TESTS

Contrary to what students believe, teachers do not create tests to use up time or seek revenge. Evaluation is an important part of the total curriculum. Test results provide measures of progress for the student, the teacher, and the parent. Tests also provide information about concepts mastered or those that require review and reteaching.

Test writing should be viewed as a continuous process. No test is perfect; there is always room for revision from year to year.

Begin planning evaluation when you structure the unit. As you list your objectives and decide how to teach the material, consider what kind of evaluation best suits the unit. If you teach a lab science, a lab test is more valid than an objective test. A music class evaluation could include performance or listening exercises. Writing progress is better judged by evaluating the writing than a mechanics worksheet.

Once you have listed the major concepts you will be presenting, and have decided on the types of evaluations, begin listing possible questions. Don't worry about the answers at this point. For each objective, list five to ten possible questions. The number of questions should be directly proportional to the time spent teaching that concept.

When you begin writing your exam, head the test clearly and provide a name space if students are to write answers on the test paper. Write specific directions. If necessary, add statements about the use of dictionaries, notes, or study cards. Let students know how much each question is worth. Create a test that is easy to read. Your test should appear professional. Word processing programs make test writing easier with quick-indent features, spell checkers, grammar checkers, and storage ability. Rewriting tests, creating alternate versions of tests, and creating make-up tests are made easier by the computer's memory and blocking functions.

Another source for unit and chapter tests is the publisher-prepared test available with your textbook. Use it with discretion. Look over each item carefully. Make sure that the questions don't violate basic test-writing techniques and that they test material you emphasized in class. Such a test usually works best when you mix the prepared questions with original questions of your own. No matter what kind of test you write, give students practice before their first graded test.

Multiple Choice

When constructing multiple-choice questions, write answer choices that are grammatically logical and parallel. First, here is an example of a poorly written multiple-choice question:

The three planets closest to the sun are:
   A. Mars Mercury and Pluto [Needs punctuation.]
   B. Saturn but not Mercury [Items are not grammatically parallel to the other choices.]
   C. Venus, Mercury, and Earth [This correct response does not support the use of the mnemonic device science teachers often employ to help students remember the planets: "My Very Efficient. . . ."]
   D. Not able to sustain life [Not parallel to the other answers in content.]

This is a better version of this test item:

The three planets closest to the sun are:
   A. Mars, Mercury, and Pluto
   B. Saturn, Mercury, and Venus
   C. Mercury, Venus, and Earth
   D. Mars, Mercury, and Venus

Your next question could address the concept of which planets support life.

Be aware of common multiple-choice test-writing pitfalls that give the answer away to test-smart students whether they know the content or not.

1. If one choice is noticeably longer than the others, it is often the answer.
2. The correct answer is frequently in the third or fourth position.
3. If you use a fifth distractor only occasionally and it is "all of the above," it is often the answer.
4. If you use one silly, nonsense distractor because you can't think of four legitimate distractors, you give your students a 25 percent gift. (And that's okay occasionally.)
5. If you include material not covered in class as an answer possibility, students will know it is not the answer.

Some multiple-choice test sections start by listing all of the possible answers. Directions instruct students to use these answers when responding to all the questions in that section. For example:

Use the following 5 answers to respond to the first 20 questions on your Chapter 2 chemistry test:
  A. hydrogen sulfide
  B. sulfur dioxide
  C. ammonia
  D. hydrogen peroxide
  E. iron oxide

Students find it frustrating to have to refer back to the first page after reading each question, so if this section of the test goes beyond one page, relist the five responses at the top of each new page. This format is especially difficult for some kinds of learners. If you do choose to use this format, be sure to write the directions clearly and state that answers can be used more than once.

True-False Items

Certain factors affect the best guessing odds on the true-false test sections.

1. Teachers traditionally include more true than false items, so guessing true gives the students better than 50 percent odds for a correct guess.
2. Words such as *always, never,* and *only* mark false questions.
3. Words such as *something, usually,* and *mostly* mark true statements.

True-false tests can be frustrating for students when:

1. All the items are true or all the items false. Such patterns are easier for students to figure out and allow them to get points without displaying knowledge.
2. A minor detail, name, or reversed date is inserted to make the item false. This technique tests visual discrimination rather than knowledge.
3. Typographical errors or poorly constructed sentences cause confusion.
4. Students are asked to mark statements with anything other that the word *true* (x, +) or *false* (0, –). Instead of accepting symbols, require that the students write out the words *true* or *false.* This forestalls the clever youngster who uses the *tralse,* a letter that a student can claim is a *T* or *F* as needed. If you find that the letters are quicker to check than the word, you might prefer that students write only a *T* or *F.* If so, make it very clear that you will need to distinguish easily between the two letters and if you can't, that the answer will be marked incorrect.

Matching

When you are constructing matching sections, it's best if each column contains no more than ten items. If you have more that ten items, create two or more sections. Each section focuses on a different type of information: vocabulary, terminology, or dates, for example. In the directions, tell students whether every answer can be used only once or if it can be used more often.

Fill-in-the-Blank

These items may be difficult for students and especially frustrating for those susceptible to test jitters if a list of terms does not accompany the items. Fill-in-the-blank items are recall questions that do not test higher levels of thinking. They do test skills such as vocabulary comprehension. Decide what you are actually testing.

Essay and Short-Answer Questions

Short-answer items test student recall and are similar to fill-in-the-blank but require the student to come up with a more complete answer. State how many responses will earn credit: "Give three examples. . . ." Directions should state whether complete sentences are required and how many points will be awarded for the content and how many, if any, will be deducted for mechanical and spelling errors. By definition, an essay question requires a response in the form of a sentence, a paragraph, or paragraphs. Before you assign an essay question on a test, write out an answer to your own question. If you have a hard time producing an answer, rewrite the question.

Essay questions test three skills simultaneously: knowledge, organization, and writing skills. If you do not wish to evaluate spelling, mechanical, or writing skills, ask for the information in the form of a diagram, drawing, list, or outline. If you are not going to evaluate mechanics, tell the students their response will earn points if you can read it. If you want your students to write strong essay responses, you have to write clear, thought-provoking questions and teach students how to write an essay.

During a review session, or in a separate lesson on how to write essay responses, show students what you expect to see in a full-point response. List verbs normally used in essay questions in your content area and discuss what each verb means. Some examples follow:

illustrate—give examples or actually draw the response

tell—use a conversational, narrative writing style

define—without using the original work, write an extended description

explain—give three or more examples

trace—arrange the response in chronological order

list—give information in a column

outline—use formal outlining techniques

conclude—give arguments and lead up to the final statement

summarize—give a broad overview of the main points

compare—tell the similarities

contrast—discuss the differences

identify—give characteristics that make the concepts different or related

To teach organizational skills, give students a scrambled list including broad topics and supporting details that are related. Students then organize these phrases, identifying broad topics and details in preparation for writing. Teach students to do "thumbnail outlines." After they read the essay question, they scribble ideas in a small box that they draw to the side of the writing area. Next, they go back through that list and number the ideas in the order of importance. Now they are ready to begin the writing of the essay response. If students are faced with several essay questions and little writing time, creating these small "thumbnail sketches" can show a teacher that the ideas were there, but the student did not have time to complete the response. This alone might earn some points, where a completely blank space will earn none.

If you want to give a mid-term or semester test that includes essay responses, but there is little time between the testing time and when grades are due, you could:

1. Administer the essay portion of the exam a week early so you have ample grading time. Give the objective portion during the formal testing period.
2. Ask for essay responses to be in the form of lists, drawings, outlines, or maps rather than paragraphs.
3. Have students write in paragraph form, but have them circle the main idea and underline supporting details.

Creating Test Versions

Essay tests are not especially conducive to cheating, but objective tests are. Giving two versions of the test curtails this problem. You will want both versions to test the same concepts, yet you do not want to spend hours of time creating two entirely different instruments. Here are some quick ways to produce second versions.

1. If you begin with a matching section followed by a multiple-choice, put the multiple-choice section first in the second version and renumber.
2. If you have more than one matching section, reverse their placement in the test.
3. Reverse the test—question for question—and renumber.
4. Keep the questions in the same order, but change the order of the answer possibilities.
5. Many teachers are beginning to include small illustrations or jokes on their tests. This relieves stress for your more visual learners. Putting different cartoons at the top of different tests shows students that there are two

test versions so they won't waste their time trying to cheat or straining their eyeballs.

6. Photocopying each test version onto two different colored papers and telling students there are two versions discourages cheating and helps you make sure no tests leave the room. If you are using answer sheets, make sure the students put their test number on the answer sheet, too.

Make-Up Tests

If you have not yet returned the test to the class, you can probably use the same test on the day the absent student returns to class. If you stored your test on a computer disk, you can construct a third version of the test by rearranging the sections and changing the essay questions. (When students steal a test to help a classmate, the absent student memorizes the answers in that test order but does not learn the answers, so he or she cannot use them to answer questions in a different order.) Some teachers save company-prepared tests for make-up, while other teachers trade tests on the same units and use the colleague's test for make-up. Neither of these two solutions is ideal because neither truly reflects what has occurred in your class.

Certain students will "cut" consistently on test days. If this is avoidance reaction due to test anxiety, a conference with a counselor might help the student deal with the stress. If the cut is to get test information from other students, a tougher make-up test cures this habit. A multiple-choice test can be quickly converted into a fill-in-the-blank test. It will test the same information but severely tax the lazy student.

GRADING TESTS

When you are grading your tests, watch for items that most of the students get wrong. If you are using computer or electronic grading aids, the machine can analyze the responses and indicate those that most students missed or that everyone got correct. You can collect this same data if you score the tests yourself. If you have an item that did not work, throw it out; do not count it as part of the grade for any student. If you tell students that you discarded a question and tell them the response you did want, you still achieve your purpose: You are making students aware of important information. You are also demonstrating to students that you are fair.

Curving grades can spark long philosophical discussions in the teachers' lounge. You might curve a test that was obviously beyond your students' abilities. You might curve to bring the point value of a test to 100 percent. You might choose to not curve at all. If several students get more than 90 percent correct, your test is probably constructed for the class learning level. You don't want to get a reputation with students of being a teacher who curves the test to passing grades no matter how poorly students do. That will take away their incentive to study. Conversely, don't make tests so difficult that no one can do well.

Handing tests back and reviewing them can be a chance to reteach, reinforce concepts, and boost student self-esteem. If you asked for essay or short-answer responses, keep track as you are grading of which students wrote good responses. As the class reviews the test, call on a variety of different students to read their answers aloud. This is extra praise for the student and lets others hear ways to answer the questions. It also gives you a chance to call on a shy or slower student who wrote a thoughtful response but usually doesn't volunteer in class. You might ask the students to rename the main points of the unit based on the questions on the test. This provides reinforcement for the central concepts before you go on to the next unit.

If a student thinks a question was graded wrong, have that student circle the item on the test and mark on the front page "recheck questions 13, 16." You can go over these problems when it is quiet. Everyone is fallible. You will make mistakes when grading or figuring scores.

If a class debates a test item, ask the students to get their notes and texts and find the citation to prove their point. They might be right, or they might prove themselves wrong, but they've done their own research. When he was in high school himself, Bill found that a teacher had missed marking eight points wrong on a test. Bill pointed out that fact to the teacher. The teacher agreed and promptly dropped Bill's grade from an A to a B. Bill never again pointed out such errors to a teacher, but as a teacher himself has urged students to point out such mistakes, knowing he will never deduct points. He sends the message to his students that testing is a learning situation for all involved. If students notice such errors, they are learning the right answers in the process.

CONCLUSION

You make curriculum decisions to meet learning objectives for the day, the unit, the semester, and the school year. Those decisions must be creative and appeal to the learning styles of individual students. They must reflect your personal teaching style and meet the requirements of the district. You set up daily and unit lessons, plus a substitute folder, based on these concepts. You enrich your curriculum with well-prepared activities that help students make connections between the concepts and their own lives. You construct a variety of evaluations that assess what students learned. Every curriculum decision you make, whether it concerns a daily activity or unit test, affects how students learn.

chapter five

Curriculum: Implementation

My advice for new teachers is:

Emily Lyman
per. 4

Use things in your teaching that we can relate to. Everything goes over our heads if you don't.

Involve us. I've had a lot of experience with student teachers. They are new at teaching, too. It's so much easier to get into the class and understand if we are participating.

Never just talk. That's not how we learn. Make it as fun as possible.

Barbara recalls several years ago when she was sermonizing to a group of yawning ninth graders about the importance of placing commas around appositives. Barbara and her class were stewing in the first stages of spring fever. The students had just been given back their latest essays, and their papers bled with comments. But even low mechanics grades were not motivation enough for rapt attention.

Barbara watched for signs of eager learners: faces turned upward, nodding; pens gripped, writing furiously; a wave of raised hands. One blonde in the back row jerked her frizz-permed head in an effort to stay awake; her eyes rolled in pre-REM stages. The boy in the seat by the window counted on his fingers. His total matched the number of times the custodian emptied his grass-catcher bag. Another young man watched, fascinated, as a spider rappelled from his tennis shoe.

Barbara slapped her chalk on the front desk, jolting the young man who occupied it back to Earth. An expletive escaped his mouth. She eyed the room wearily. "I swear, I could stand up here on my head naked and I still don't think you'd pay attention." Giggles and titters. One boy who aspired to be a casino dealer in Las Vegas spoke up.

"Yeah, we would," he drawled, "for maybe five minutes."

Like Barbara, you will have days when the struggle to engage your students' interest is monumental. You'll also have days, especially if you are a new teacher, that seem to be consumed with classroom management and discipline. The best way to avoid or eliminate these problems of restlessness, inattentiveness, and misbehavior is through effective curriculum presentation. Your aim is to develop teaching practices that engage every student. Then, when you face a situation like Barbara's, you'll be prepared to switch strategies in midstream and respark your students' interest.

CLEAR DIRECTIONS

Students can be auditory, visual, or tactile learners. Most students seem to comprehend better if they both hear and see the information presented. It's for this reason that students should see directions on an overhead, handout, computer/TV monitor, board, or in the text while you explain the directions orally. This way, they both hear and see the material—making stronger connections. Any writing students do while taking notes, copying assignments, or drafting responses then reinforces learning.

An ideal way to reinforce directions is to model or demonstrate the process you want students to follow, or to show samples of possible products. For example, math teachers solve sample problems on the board before students begin working independently. English teachers use early drafts of essays to show students the process of revision. Volleyball coaches demonstrate proper spikes and sets.

Although it's important for students to understand what's expected of them, showing models does have its drawbacks. The model may inhibit divergent thinking. Students may perceive that the model you show represents exactly what you require. For this reason, give more creative assignments without a model.

Your directions must be clear. You'll grow exhausted repeating yourself. The most frustrating questions you'll hear are those that follow an explanation you believe is concise. It's a good idea to check periodically for student comprehension. As you make specific points, giving directions or demonstrations, ask the students to tell you what's going on.

- "Tell the class in your own words what each of you must accomplish at home tonight so we can do the science experiment tomorrow, Jamie."
- "On this slip of paper, I want you to write down the topic of your essay and three arguments you will use to prove your thesis."
- "As you begin your silent reading, I will walk past each desk and check to make sure you understand the assignment."
- "Will you tell the class what pages to read tonight, Kelly? . . . Is she right, Andy?"

QUESTIONING STUDENTS

Teachers commit numerous errors when asking questions. One common mistake is to state a student's name before the question: "Sally, what's the answer to question 7?" The problem with this technique is that Sally is put on the spot before she even knows the question, much less the answer, while the other twenty-five students are immediately off the hook. "Why think when I don't have to?" is the silent response of many. Ask a question, pause, and allow time for twenty-six minds to search for an answer before calling on Sally to respond. You might also call on one or two others to validate Sally's answer; then ask the rest of the class to nod or raise their hands if they agree. You can use these techniques even if you have asked a question requiring a single, specific response.

Many curriculum topics allow for questions that might elicit a variety of answers rather than a single correct one. You might use these open-ended questions because several students can respond instead of just one. Tell students to think about the question you are about to ask without raising hands or speaking. This allows everyone to focus. Ask the question. Then ask several students to share their thoughts. If a student pauses at the end of a statement, don't assume he or she is finished. Wait a few seconds before calling on someone else. Often the first student has more to add and is pausing to organize thoughts. During discussions you might ask a student to record individual responses on the board. After six or seven answers, call on one student to summarize. If you like quiet and order, require raised hands, but wait before you call on the first student. The object is to provide enough time for everyone to *think* of a response. Mentally count to five to make sure you allow that time.

If a student gives an inaccurate answer, you might ask another question to clarify: "Do you mean 1990 or 1890?" Another strategy is to provide the question that correlates with the student's incorrect answer. While Robert was reviewing directions for a math assignment, he asked, "What kind of problems require a quotient for an answer?" A student answered, "Multiplication problems." Robert dignified the response: "Products are the answers to multiplication problems. We're still dealing with sets. What kind of problems yield quotients?" In this statement Robert linked the student response with the correct question, then tried a new prompt to get the desired answer. If a student has no response, say you will come back to her or him. This holds the student accountable for listening more carefully to other responses. You might ask a student to paraphrase or summarize previous answers.

The way you acknowledge a response is critical. *Never* humiliate a student. While sarcasm is often tempting, such negative reactions may come back to haunt you. For most correct answers a simple "Good" or "Great" may be adequate. Non-verbal acknowledgments such as a nod or wink serve the same purpose. If the answer is a winner, an "Excellent, John" may be appropriate. If the answer is not complete, respond by saying something like, "You're on the right track; can anyone take Ryan's idea further?"

CLOWNS AND RINGMASTERS

Occasionally you'll be blessed with a clown who believes that you and your class live for his or her witty comments. Sometimes a dose of nonthreatening humor will silence the offender. A smile at the student and a short "Not today" may do the trick. Often, ignoring the remark and concentrating on the responses from the rest of the class will solve the problem. Usually the primary goal of this student is attention, and the sooner you can deal with the behavior, the better. If ignoring or making light of the situation doesn't work and the comedian continues the act, you could move toward the student, use a stern tone saying, "Sean, that's enough!" and proceed. If the offender still persists, you're probably ready to look at the student, state "I'll see you after class," and proceed with the discipline/classroom management steps.

Especially when you are a new teacher, you may encounter the youngster who wants to be viewed as "The Authority" by pointing out misspelled words, incorrect references, and grammatical slips. This individual likes to flaunt self-proclaimed brilliance. The goal is to catch you unprepared or without an answer. If this student begins to dominate the discussion, you could acknowledge the student's obvious interest in the topic and make this person the "research authority." The student's job is to listen quietly and serve as backup authority. This student gets attention, yet others have opportunities to respond. Be sure to use this "authority" to double-check answers or summarize from time to time.

Sometimes students ask questions with the best of intentions, and you honestly don't know the answer. Admit you don't know and suggest an investigation. Either name a source for the information requested or attempt to find it yourself. Often the student doesn't require an explanation as detailed as the one you will provide, but she or he and the rest of the class will see that you want to learn with them.

If you are well prepared, the attempts to trip you will fail and students won't wish to expend the energy pointlessly challenging you. Don't discourage challenges, though. Show students that intellectual curiosity and questioning are part of the lively learning climate you like in your classes.

RELEVANCE

Much of what teachers present in the classroom doesn't seem to have relevance to students. It is your task to assist students in making connections, even if the connection is as simple as "Yesterday, when we finished reading *Sarah, Plain and Tall,* I understood why Sarah felt lonely. Have you ever felt lonely? Today we're going to discuss and write about what to do when we feel alone." As an effective teacher, you must demonstrate the *why* of learning. Some subjects and lessons lend themselves to this. It's not difficult for the aspiring engineer to see the relevance of math, the future attorney the benefits of debate, or the contractor the importance of drafting. For the classes or lessons that don't appeal to students, for one reason or another, it's critical that you demonstrate relevance and personal enthusiasm. One afternoon, Betty was introducing Edgar Allan Poe in a junior American lit class. From the back of the room, a red-haired girl who was prone to

Free Advice

gum-popping whined, "Why do we hafta learn this? I'm gonna be a bag lady." She grinned at the boy next to her. Betty informed her that Poe was a master of the macabre, wrote excessively on themes of premature burial, insanity, and revenge. She could sense that she had related to a few in the room. Betty continued, explaining the connections between Poe and Stephen King, which sparked a few comments like "Yeah, like the Usher House and the Overlook in *The Shining.*" Betty continued, smiling at the young lady, "Poe often haunted the streets himself. He was found unconscious in an alley one night. Three days later, he died." The redhead quit chewing her gum.

FLEXIBILITY AND PACING

You need to consider critical thinking, cooperative learning, and problem solving in classroom planning. Allowing time for individual work is equally important. Some students work best if they're left alone; others need interaction—if not for boosting their own wavering self-esteem, then for the simple release of energy. You are not an evil teacher if you allow students to read a poem aloud in pairs, look up answers as a team, or use a colored crayon instead of a pen or pencil. Effective classroom management requires variety. Ideally, activities should change every fifteen to twenty-five minutes, depending on the age and maturity of the students. Here are some suggestions to infuse your class time with variety:

- If students have been reading for twenty minutes, have them stop briefly to discuss or write about what they are reading.
- If you've been lecturing for twenty-five minutes, stop and give students time to peruse their notes and exchange ideas with a classmate.
- If students have been playing math games in small groups, call them together so they can all view the board or screen. Lead a large-group activity, focusing on the concept used to play the games. This could be a demonstration, board work, or role-playing. After you've assessed student comprehension, give directions for the day's independent practice. Allow the remaining twenty minutes for quiet, uninterrupted work time.

There are, of course, exceptions. When you have a deadline for a film return or the teacher down the hall is pleading for the room set of books you're currently using, every minute is critical. If you explain this dilemma to students, they are usually cooperative about a change in scheduling.

Flexibility is also critical in giving assignments—both in creating them and in interpreting them. If you know your objectives, you should, in many cases, offer a variety of options to your students for achieving these objectives. Students participate better when they're allowed choices, such as:

- In a science class, consider several methods to achieve the same goal. For example, in a cooperative team, one student might take the flower apart while the second draws. The third student might talk about what he or she is seeing, while the fourth records it in a field journal.

- In math class, offer a variety of problems and allow the students to choose among them, or have pairs act out story problems.
- Use task cards, with the students choosing among different activities in a category.
- List as many as ten writing options. The students complete one or two.
- On the essay portion of a test, list several questions that test the same skill. Let students choose which to answer.

Obviously, options are not always appropriate, but whenever possible, incorporate them. Assignment choices can stretch student minds beyond simple recall into sophisticated thinking.

DEALING WITH DISTRESSING EVENTS

The need for flexibility in the classroom surfaces in another way: as a response to current events. When a particularly grisly murder is splashed across the six o'clock news, fire consumes a neighborhood in your town, or a sports idol announces a terminal illness, students can talk of little else. Students need to communicate about such events, and brushing aside a disaster without some comment seems to contradict the whole point of relevance that teachers strive to achieve.

If a death of a classmate occurs, or several students are involved in a traffic accident, those moments of human experience contain a lesson. Betty had an incident with a student whose friend had committed suicide over spring break. The student announced that fact to the class, but would say no more. It was obvious that he was deeply affected and in agony. After class, Betty talked with him about his loss. She asked the school social worker to talk with him. At the time he was angry with her for interfering, but two days later apologized with a shaking voice and thanked her for her caring.

A second grader in Robert's class was the victim of a fatal car accident. Thursday she'd occupied a desk; Friday she was dead. The administrators called the parents of the other children in Robert's class, informing them of the little girl's death. They encouraged parents to talk with their children before school the next day. The class united in their displays of sympathy. They donated money for flowers and made cards for the family. Trained school personnel were available to children and parents for grief counseling. This became an important lesson to these second graders about learning to deal with the death of a friend.

Whether your students are faced with a personal tragedy or a natural disaster, be flexible and compassionate. Shift the curriculum a bit and discuss earthquakes a month earlier, or just spend a few minutes listening to students. The class will see you as human with concerns like theirs, as opposed to some android that self-destructs each day at 4:00.

When students are upset, you might have them begin an impromptu journal-write on the topic distressing them. You could do a write-it-and-tear-it-up activity to purge students' feelings of anger or fear or frustration. You might talk about appropriate and inappropriate ways people handle emotions.

You could talk about TV programs or books on similar themes. You might remind students about a piece of literature that included the theme. After being given this opportunity to express and share their concerns, your students should begin to calm down and refocus on the current lesson.

After the crisis, talk with colleagues about what happened. They will relate stories of similar experiences, and you can store their solutions in your mind for future use.

REFOCUSING AFTER INTERRUPTIONS

Besides the usual interruptions of messages, call slips, and announcements over the intercom discussed in Chapter 4, assemblies for student government, upcoming games, health education, and cultural enrichment will disrupt your daily routine. Multiday, schoolwide testing schedules will also break the flow of your lessons. In short, unexpected interruptions will sabotage your best-planned learning experiences.

These interruptions will happen, so don't let them upset you; just learn to adjust with good humor. Early warning helps, of course, which you'll get in the case of most assemblies and test days. As soon as your administration announces these events, write them into your lesson plan book even if the dates are months ahead.

ASSEMBLIES

Sometimes assemblies occur on short notice. Creative teachers learn ways to adjust. Once again, getting upset only hurts you. If students are to report to class for roll call before moving to the auditorium, you could use that opportunity to announce before they leave: "Since we will not work together today, I need you to read the following material at home tonight." If you want to be sure students follow through, you could add, "There will be a quiz on that reading when you walk in the door tomorrow." Also, in the few minutes when you have the class's attention before the assembly, remind the students of proper assembly manners, school pride, and maturity. They can never hear that material too often. When your students return to class, you might spend some time discussing what happened in the assembly (good or bad) and why schools have assemblies. This is an opportunity to talk about large-group behavior. Ask students how assembly etiquette might apply to other situations in their lives. Ask how school assemblies are the same or different from professional ball games, rock concerts, and parades. Write down questions like these before class. This discussion will run most smoothly if organized by prewritten prompts on the topic of assembly behavior that you've thought through ahead of time. It's best not to "wing it."

Sometimes parts of one class or several classes are affected by assemblies or other interruptions and others aren't. If you want to get your classes back in sync, assign drawing, writing, or reading activities related to what you've been working on in class. This will allow you to do something different in the classes that you do meet, and you won't have to play "catch up" later on. On the other hand, different classes will have different levels of interest in the same topic, so being at different places in the curriculum in different classes is perfectly appropriate if you prefer that approach.

TESTING DAYS

Many districts administer achievement tests at specific grade levels for four or five days. Last year, Betty taught her juniors the first two periods, tested thirty juniors (not all her usual students) for 110 minutes, the equivalent of two periods, for five consecutive days, ate lunch, and taught her last two periods. These test schedules are hard on the kids and hard on you. Here are some specific things to keep in mind (rather than losing it) when doing several-day testing:

The students will be emotionally tired in the classes where tests are not being administered. Do not give unit exams or have major assignments due at this time.

- Plan activities in class that change frequently and involve student movement, small group work, planned group responses, and a bit of fun. You can still cover the concepts, but you need to plan for students' active (physical and mental) participation to distract them from their testing fatigue.
- You might plan a half-day lesson on test-taking strategies. Include relaxation techniques. Talk about how you handled tense testing situations in college. Tell your students about taking the National Teacher Exam or the district technology exam. Talk about test anxiety and discuss your own strategies for dealing with that cold fist gripping your insides and freezing your brain.
- Plan alternative methods for teaching. Betty taught a short story unit lasting the duration of the testing days in the classes she did meet and culminated with a film of the short story the day she had all her classes back. The students involved in testing saw the film their first day back. This caught them up with the other classes and gave them a rewarding visual break while helping them mentally get ready to return to regular class routine.
- Don't schedule free time. This quickly disintegrates into a free-for-all and a management nightmare.

UNEXPECTED EVENTS/ STUDENT REMOVAL

Sometimes classroom lightning strikes not once but several times in a period and the lesson stalls: The Internet link is full and your students' access is blocked. The VCR eats the tape. The computer simulation will take fifty minutes and you have just been informed that the buses will arrive twenty minutes late because of snow. How do you manage the lesson and keep students focused?

You might say, after distraction number 379, "I've lost my train of thought. Help me. What were we talking about? What do you have last in your notes? Let's go to page 156 in your text and pick up the concept this simulation would have taught and then you'll be ready to start the minute you get to class tomorrow." These questions and statements can help refocus your students and you.

One type of interruption that is certain to destroy students' attention is when an administrator or resource officer arrives at your door to remove a student from your class without warning. Having a student pulled out of class is disturbing for you and the other students. Even if you have worked hard to establish a trusting, safe environment, these abrupt actions ruin that safe feeling. If a student does have to be pulled out of class, ask the authorities on the scene to deal with the student down the hall, out of sight and earshot of your classroom. If your students are particularly disturbed by what's happening to their classmate, point out that you have no more information than they do. If they get back to the lesson, the class period will seem to go faster. They all know they will get the "full story" in the halls between classes.

CREATIVE LESSON PLANNING IDEAS

Begin building a file of techniques you can use for review no matter what you are teaching. You might use some of these exercises in the beginning of the period to help students actively review the previous day's lesson or focus their attention on the new material. You might use other short activities at the end of the period to reinforce concepts and fill the last minutes of class.

You can gather these techniques by listening to other teachers, attending share fairs, observing colleagues, or reading professional magazines.

Here are some ideas for activities in specific curriculum areas.

Language Arts

- Hand the students a sheet of unlined 8 × 11 paper and have them draw the house of a favorite character in the story you are studying, draw the path of a character's movement through the story, or illustrate the symbols or theme in the story. Have students share their work and base evaluation on amount of detail and symbolism rather than artistic talent.

- Have the students write a scene that is *not* in the story. For example, in "The Devil and Tom Walker" by Washington Irving, the conversation between the devil and Mrs. Tom Walker is not included. You will seldom get identical responses to this assignment.

- In small groups, have students plan and present a very short skit or tableau about what happens after the story ends.

- After students read E. B. White's *Stuart Little*, have them write or tell the ending to the story.

- Have students illustrate their vocabulary words.

- Have students jot down three "Why . . ." or "What if . . ." questions about the story and then ask classmates their questions. These questions elicit multiple responses, so every student answer can be correct.

Mathematics

- Have each student create, on a fresh sheet of paper, three new problems that illustrate that day's concept. Students then pass the paper two classmates to the right for computation, one classmate forward for checking, then back to the originator for scoring. Talk about what makes a good example and what does not.

- Use cooperative groups to begin homework.

- Hand each small group a different brainteaser. Each must solve the problem and then explain how they did this to the rest of the class.
- Have students measure the classroom and use these statistics to create original math problems, using the concepts being currently taught.

Science

To review lab procedures the day before doing a lab exercise, put the students into small groups and hand each a written description of a student performing a lab exercise. Have each group report to the rest of the class about what was done correctly and what should have been done differently to ensure an accurate, safe lab experience.

- Share a short essay. You might begin collecting a file of essays on science. James Thurber wrote several. Current authors who appeal to students include Barry Lopez, David Quarnmen, Annie Dillard, John McPhee, and Patrick McManus.
- Show a science-oriented cartoon. Ask what makes it funny and why.
- Have students write out "How come . . ." questions on the current topic and take turns asking class members for answers.
- Build a collection of current science magazines in your classroom. Students can browse through these periodicals, locate an article of interest, read it, and complete a short written or oral report. Just looking through current science magazines demonstrates to students that science is an ongoing field in which fresh discoveries are continually being made—a perspective of which students might otherwise lose sight.

Social Studies

- Have small groups prepare short skits of famous events from another viewpoint: V-E Day from the perspective of a German private, an old villager, or Eisenhower's assistant (a different person for each group).

■ Have students think and jot down ideas and be ready to share on the question: What person in history would you like to meet, and what would you talk about? You could limit this topic to one era, one incident, or one specific group of people. Having students write down what they are going to talk about keeps each student responsible for participating. These ideas could be the foundation for a creative writing assignment.

■ Have small groups write a specific number of questions and answers on the front and back of note cards. Then discuss and collect the cards to use at the end of the unit or the semester for a *Jeopardy*-like review game. This would also provide an opportunity to review by having students classify questions into categories and then rank those in each category by degree of difficulty.

■ Have small groups look for links or similarities between historical events and daily national, local, and school news events. You could cut paper into strips and have students write their responses on these strips and link them together around the room in a chain.

■ Speculate about what a teenager's life might have been like in the era you're studying.

Computer Science and Consumer Technology Classes

These classes used to be called manual arts, auto shop, industrial arts, wood shop, home economics, or family living. These types of classes now involve computers, simulations, and sophisticated software tool programs or community work experience as observers or interns in the workplace. The focus of the class is more closely on work than in the traditional academic classes.

Hands-on classes seldom seem to have enough time for work and cleanup. If you also need focus time, showing a student's project in progress and discussing the process could benefit other students working on similar tasks.

Music

- Keep rehearsing; let students direct.
- Have students illustrate their impressions of musical selections as they listen.
- Have students compare and contrast contemporary music with music from another period.
- Have students research a popular composer on the Internet and give a written or oral report to the class.

Physical Education

- Have small groups of students plan drills to practice specific skills safely.
- Have students perform these skill practices in slow motion or to a piece of music with a heavy, consistent beat.
- Design a multiage activity in which the older students teach skills to younger students.
- Invite a guest speaker or alternate mobility team to talk to students about the importance of fitness and determination. Students could participate in a game with this team.
- Have students research a popular sports figure and role-play the part, in an interview format.

WHEN LESSON PLANS DON'T WORK OUT

Sometimes a lesson will fall flat. Before the next class begins, ask yourself these questions:

1. Could the material be better learned cooperatively rather than individually?
2. Would your students understand the material better if you assigned small groups two questions to answer before whole-group study and discussion?
3. Would the activity be more effective after the film rather than before?

4. Would an explanation work better if you role-played? Could students stand in the configuration of the molecule, walk through the battle, or represent the parts of the story problem?
5. Can you adjust the topic to relate it more closely to the students' interest? Would a discourse on Thoreau's "Civil Disobedience" explore the same ideas if students wrote about civil disobedience today? Could the same topic be related to war protests?

What can you do when you give a wonderful lecture, complete it with a dramatic sweep of your hand, and notice blank paper and blank student faces? Try this approach: Tell your students, "Now you've heard the material. Using that information, let me show you how I would put it in my notes if I were sitting at one of your desks hearing this same lecture." Then proceed to review by writing a skeleton outline on the board, an overhead projector, or on the computer-to-TV monitor. You might draw an idea-tree or list the steps of the procedure while eliciting student prompts for your work. Ask questions as you work: "What was the next point I made? Is this a new support point or an example for the previous one? Should I put a drawing here? Would that help my notes?" Besides providing a review, this process can show students how to take notes. Study skills are not passed genetically from generation to generation. It would probably help if you could put the main points of a lecture on the board, overhead, or presentation software before class. Your preparation work will help students see the transitions.

If you have presented information and helped your students take notes, but the confusion remains, try this: Ask, "What is the one main idea of today's material? On a fresh sheet of paper, write that topic in the center. With your notes covered, write down everything you can remember about that topic." Then ask students to look over their papers and circle the three most important ideas. They might trade with a neighbor and add at least one more detail before trading back. Ask various students to read one of their circled ideas aloud. Some may be repeated, but that only reinforces importance. (This is an ideal time to call on less able students so they can give a correct response in front of peers.) Ask why the student felt the mentioned point was important. Responses reflect higher levels of thinking. This review process can also work as a focus the next day to start the lesson.

When your students just don't seem to grasp an assignment, try giving different examples and more guided practice on that concept. Ask your students if they can explain why they are having trouble with the assignment, and discuss learning techniques they could use successfully. Use the lesson to reinforce study techniques even if you have to work through the assignment step by step. Then go back and look for the central concept together.

Cooperative work can help get your students through an assignment that is difficult for them. "I can see we are all suffering. Instead of finishing these at home, be sure your name is on the paper and turn in what you have done so far. I'll score that. Tomorrow we'll review the concept and give some more examples, and you can work with two classmates to complete the activity. I'll score this revision." Sharing answers and working together can be a positive technique. You can structure work sessions that begin with individual effort and later move to group effort for both reinforcement and review.

If students are struggling with a tough reading assignment, pair them up and have them read aloud to each other. At the bottom of each page, the pair should stop, talk about what they read, summarize the main ideas, and write them in their notes. This is a noisy activity, but everyone is involved in seeking meaning. During the last ten minutes of class, call students to order and have them share their notes. Then, based on their notes and listening, have them summarize the main ideas.

You might want to have a short worksheet, essay, or quiz as an alternative if disaster strikes and the lesson simply doesn't work no matter what you do. You may prepare this extra lesson segment and not need to use it. However, file it away for future use.

You can minimize lesson flops by always staying focused on the unit or concept you are teaching and planning everything you do in your classroom to relate to the teaching and reinforcement of that concept.

If you know you are usually an effective teacher, don't take an occasional disappointing lesson too much to heart. Students are caught up in their own worlds and it can be hard to get them to share in your enthusiasm or concern. Lessons will bomb now and again: That's a given. But never let fear of a "disaster" keep you from trying new, creative strategies.

DEALING WITH THE TEXTBOOK

You probably won't have much time or opportunity to choose the textbook(s) you will be using. Most likely, your school will be using district-adopted texts. If you must make a choice early on, consider using the text your colleagues are using. This will make it easier to share ideas.

If you do find yourself teaching with a textbook that is too easy or too difficult, keep in close contact with fellow teachers for teaching ideas. Utilize the teacher resource center if you have access to one through your district or a nearby college.

Rather than using the textbook exclusively for your lessons, use a variety of techniques when having students deal with the reading material. The variety of approaches will appeal to a wider range of reading abilities in your classroom.

- Plan reading assignments that vary in length. Sometimes the chapter needs to be read straight through, other times it is best read in segments. You need to teach or review the necessary reading technique before they begin. Students need not read every word of a difficult text. Instead, they might read a few passages to get the general idea. Use other media to enrich the printed material: You could view a video, bring in a guest speaker, create a trivia-style game, or use a computer simulation.
- Have students work with a friend, reading aloud or silently, then take notes together after each section or paragraph.
- Make a game out of the chapter vocabulary. Introduce the vocabulary first. Have students act out the meanings, then review and test the students later. Students might create their own games to reinforce vocabulary by using computer software. Students could also illustrate vocabulary words.
- If your students' reading abilities warrant it, ask the reading specialist to come in and demonstrate prereading skills and techniques while you watch. Then reinforce these skills for *every* reading assignment. Practice these skills on easier material first.
- Teach your students to use the summary at the end of the chapter and the review questions as a prereading device. Don't just tell the students to read these parts on their own. Read them together in class and discuss what students might learn in the chapter. Model the techniques you want the students to use.
- Tell your students what they are going to read about before they begin. Pique student interest by referring to the mysteries in the story: the main character's unknown past; the conflict that triggers irreversible decisions; the clues that lead to the surprising climax. However, *never* tell the ending. Tell your students that

you took a vow when you became a teacher *never* to reveal conclusions.

■ Write the characters' names on the board with an identifying phrase or pictograph for each. Have students copy and keep the list for quick reference during the reading.

■ Study guides focus on the important concepts in the reading. For every fourth or fifth item, add "Why" or "What if" questions that can only be answered after reflection.

Do not conduct round-robin reading sessions. They do not make good use of learning time. This method puts inappropriate stress on the poor oral reader, lets those not reading off the hook, and bores the faster readers to tears. When introducing a novel, however, you might read the first chapter aloud and have the class work through the first study questions together. When students begin to get interested in the book, let them continue silently at their own best pace. Every few days at the beginning of the period, have students identify which page they are reading. This assures the slower students that they are not alone and gives everyone incentive to manage remaining reading time. It also helps you plan for the next part of the presentation.

If you are starting students on a science or social studies chapter, model being the student yourself. Read the first paragraph or section aloud and then pose questions to yourself about what will come next in the chapter. Ask your students these questions. Then let the students read on to find the answers. You might break the entire chapter up into small chunks and lead the students through one section at a time.

Encourage your students to outline, take notes, and interpret the text on their own, but help them through the process. Merely handing out a summary will not help the students use the book independently. Prepare an outline and then delete headings, lists of details, or vocabulary words.

Students can then fill in the missing information as they read.

Teacher's guides often indicate how to modify lessons for various abilities. These modifications may include shortened word lists, altered math assignments, or guidelines for creating appropriate essay questions. Other support materials that may accompany texts are transparencies, computer software, audio- and videocassettes, laser disks, posters for discussion, math manipulatives, and suggestions for enrichment activities that reinforce the central concepts of the text. Ask colleagues in your school or department if these materials are available. Be sure to check in your school media center. They may be stored there or in another central area. Sometimes a phone call to your publisher's local representative is all it takes to obtain some of these items.

DIFFICULT TEACHING ASSIGNMENTS

When you sign a contract, you usually have a clear idea about what subjects you will teach. However, difficulties can arise when, in the course of the teaching year, your workload seems to extend beyond what even a computer can handle.

This is most likely to happen to you during your first year of teaching or your first year in a new assignment or building. The first assignment in any setting can be overwhelming to anyone. Five years ago, Marc accepted a position that he knew would include slow-learning seniors. He taught five classes of thirty-two to thirty-six slow or lazy learners who had convinced the counselors they needed an "easy" class. These classes had no texts and no specific curriculum, and there were no other math teachers on Marc's floor. The students in one class frequently bragged to Marc how many teachers they had caused to quit. When the burden of a tough teaching assignment begins to weigh upon you, try a few of the following strategies.

Change one thing at a time. Make a list of what is going well and what is most overwhelming. Identify the first thing you'd like to change. If discipline needs to improve, plan highly structured daily lessons. Start each lesson with a journal-write, quiz, or story problem. This will give you time to take accurate roll and focus the students on the lesson. When your students realize you are there to teach, most will go along with the plan. For those who do not comply, it is critical that you begin to implement a discipline plan.

Consult with colleagues. Experienced teachers can give you advice and suggestions for coping with your workload. If you are a beginning teacher, get to know the other new teachers. You might form a mutual support group and, in the process, find out you all are doing better than you thought.

Assigning written work is one way to hold your students accountable for what you are teaching. However, you must be able to cope with all the papers they produce. To do so, try some of these ideas:

- Have students exchange papers and score them. This is a valid way to reinforce correct answers.
- Have students answer five questions each day on a twenty-question worksheet and hand the paper in at the end of the hour. You need only to put a check mark in the margin where they finished and return the paper the next day. Grade it on the fourth day.
- Grade daily work on the plus, check, minus system: + = assignment done exceptionally well; ✓ = assignment done, full credit; – = assignment turned in, not completed. You can group students' papers into these three general categories without reading each item word for word. You might record all plus/check/minus grades on one sheet and then assign one overall homework grade to students' daily papers at the end of the grading period.

- After determining grading criteria, peruse each student paper without marking individual errors and assign a grade. Evaluate the next assignment with comments so students can learn from their work.
- A real dilemma is grading for mechanics and spelling errors. One quick way to accomplish this is to place a check mark in the margin of the line in which the error occurs. This alerts the student to check the line for a spelling or mechanics problem and requires students to be responsible for their own learning. If your students are using computers to complete written assignments, teach them how to use the spell- and grammar-check features.
- Skim for key phrases and stack the papers in piles, depending on how each paper compares with others in quality and completeness.
- Have students trade essay responses. You need to identify on the overhead, board, or TV monitor what students are to check for in their peers' work: for example, underlining main ideas, circling spelling errors, and checking where punctuation is needed. This will serve as a prereading aid for you.
- Have your students outline some essay answers rather than write prose. Take time to review the outlining rules; don't expect the students to remember the skill from previous years.
- Have students trade papers and, with a colored pencil, underline the main ideas or supporting details.
- As the students work, walk past each desk, making helpful suggestions or pointing out answers you especially like. Then put a check mark on the paper and in your grade book as a record of having seen that assignment. At the end of the period, students need only to file these papers in their notebooks. Encourage students to keep these quick-grade assignments by allowing them to use such papers when taking quizzes.

In the beginning of the year, your paper load tends to be heavier. There are reasons for this. You need to see student work to assess abilities, spot students in need of special help, and learn if each student understands what you are trying to teach. You might also gain information about the amount of background that your students have in your subject area. As you and your class begin functioning as a team, you will find ways of lessening this load. You will also find you do not need to collect work from each student every day to keep the students on task.

If you feel your teaching assignment is overwhelming because of the amount of material that needs to be presented on a topic, consider using groups. Place students in learning groups, providing the material or helping them find it in the media center. Give specific tasks for each group to accomplish. Each group then presents what they've learned about the topic, giving you breathing time. Your job is still to present the introductory material and the main concepts of the units, but students can contribute the supplementary information. You then correct misconceptions and reinforce main concepts. When the groups are presenting their material, keep the rest of the class responsible for what they hear by taking notes yourself and including the material on your next test. This process can also model good note taking for your students, so let them see your written comments. In the margin, jot down possible test questions, key phrases, and vocabulary. You might write your notes on the overheads or by using the keyboard of the PC-to-TV setup. Discuss both the material and your note-taking techniques with students.

When you teach, you are functioning on at least three levels simultaneously: classroom management, content, and method of presentation. Should you feel you're about to explode if you have to deal with one more detail, consider dealing with only one of these three main areas at a time. Teach a topic that's easier for you so you can concentrate on the discipline. Fall back on what's familiar. Cut back on paperwork by utilizing peer-scoring techniques for some assignments or requesting oral responses. Read the chapter on wellness.

INCLUSION IN THE CLASSROOM

Every time a teacher prepares to greet a class for the first time, he or she is filled with the expectation that all students will be motivated, eager, and intelligent. That reality does not exist. Classrooms are filled with children displaying different learning abilities, different methods of coping, and different personal goals. Hidden in these same children are issues of gender, race, and social history that combine to affect the response of each child to each learning task. There is no way one carefully planned lesson will be perceived or learned in the same manner by all students in the room.

A professional educator's goal is to help students learn. In recent years this goal has become increasingly difficult to achieve. Classrooms are filled with diverse student abilities. Today's teachers face classes of wide-ranging reading levels: Very poor, sometime homeless students who come to school because it provides warmth, food, or safety sit next to students tanned from a family trip to Disneyland. Still other students might have recently returned from a hospital stay for depression, from juvenile detention, or from the other parent in another state. Substance abuse, teenage pregnancy, or suppressed anger add other dimensions to this diverse collection of individuals.

The reality is that students of all abilities and backgrounds have the legal right to be included in the American classroom. Another reality is that teachers seldom feel prepared to handle the diversity now regularly found in their classrooms. But this reality also does not mean that a teacher is expected to write individual lesson plans for students with different needs, nor does it mean that students work out of textbooks written on different reading levels. Teachers can build inclusive teaching techniques into everyday lessons in such a way that students can enjoy successes and the teaching load does not increase.

Inclusive teaching is an attitude. Inclusive teachers use teaching methods that appeal to a variety of learning styles and offer students choices that increase motivation. The teacher takes the role of mentor and cheerleader, holding high expectations for all. Every student in every class must be considered a special student: Each has learning strengths and weaknesses. Each student has something unique to offer. Each student has the ability to grow and learn. Teacher education classes for teaching the gifted use most of the same techniques that are taught in special education training classes. Employing these strategies benefits all students.

When Melanie realized the diverse needs in her history class, she sought advice from her mentor. "I've watched you teach. You keep all your kids involved. The minute I stop to help Billy, Jamie is out of his seat and tugging at my sleeve."

Her mentor assured Melanie that she was on the right track; she had clear classroom expectations and was practicing good classroom management. Her mentor went on to assure Melanie that an inclusive teaching style was not a one-time epiphany—her mentor had developed his bag of tricks through years of trial and error, working with other teachers, and dialogue with colleagues. "Add one technique at a time and be comfortable with what you are doing. Don't adopt a technique I use unless it fits your own teaching style."

This experienced teacher went on to talk about curriculum. Following the district curriculum using the district materials is expected by administrators, but there are lots of things that can be done in both lesson planning and lesson preparation that will include more and more students in the learning process.

Consider planning the lesson backwards. Sound strange? But consider this approach because it moves from the concrete to the philosophical—a clear approach for students. After deciding on the next unit and its objectives, identify the final outcomes—what do the students need to know at the end of the unit? How many different ways can students show that they understand the concepts? How will students practice the material before the final grades are assigned? What kind of practice can they do as groups and independently? What information has to be presented for students to begin their practice? Once this information is identified—material, guided practice, feedback, independent practice, evaluation—you can plan a logical lesson that reviews the previous material and leads into the new material. This "backwards" planning provides a clear, linear lesson plan for both teacher and student.

Inclusion Techniques

A clear lesson plan allows for clear directions. Different students need to hear the directions, or see the directions on the board or in closer focus on paper. Others need to write the directions down or repeat the expectations to the teacher, a classmate, or an adult assistant. Giving directions this way involves different learning styles using different senses. Some students work best when handed an outline with spaces for key words or phrases. Others can concentrate and take effective notes from an overhead projector or presentation software. Pausing can both allow time for slower writers to keep pace and emphasize important points for those who need to strengthen their listening skills. Gifted students might be challenged to listen without writing until a pause or a prearranged signal and then write a summary in their notebook.

The next inclusive step is to begin offering choices during practice sessions. Students who can choose methods of practice and reporting will be more motivated and feel power over their learning. During practice, students might opt to work alone, with a partner or group, or with an adult assistant. A simple choice such as being able to stretch out on the floor while working is an inclusive option that pleases some students who find confinement to desks license to wiggle. Some students might do better with earphones clamped over their ears, while other classmates work best in a special needs classroom down the hall. (Many schools now have tutoring centers where all students are welcome to come and work.) The only rule of using inclusion techniques is that the teacher, student, and parents be comfortable with all the choices given and that the choices be within the rules and safety expectations of the school.

After observing her mentor's success, Melanie felt ready to try some inclusion techniques in her history class. She planned to introduce the unit on reconstruction by showing a five-minute video clip about the aftermath of the Civil War. She would introduce the main concepts of the unit by displaying an outline using presentation software. She asked students to copy the outline in their notebooks and choose one item to research. "What a deal," Melanie teased, "one-fifth the work for five-fifths the knowledge." The students, grouped by topic choice and some help from Melanie, were given a page of guidelines and time to locate information on their subtopic using the textbook, library materials, and electronic sources. Each group was charged with learning and teaching the material to classmates and each group member had to take a role. These choices gave those students who hate to recite in front of the class a chance to prepare the visual and simply stand with the group while the more verbal teammate recited the information and the computer whiz managed the multimedia program from a nearby terminal. The fourth team member was the student who liked to write and chose to complete the written notes for the classroom notebook—available to absent students for make-up work. Students not presenting their report took notes, listened, and asked clarifying questions of the presenting group.

After Melanie read more about inclusive teaching, she readjusted her grading points so that tests could not be the sole determinant of a student's grade. Melanie decided that she would feel comfortable structuring each unit so that there were points to be earned for written, creative, and auditory work. Jamie, a poor writer but talented artist, became more willing to attempt an essay knowing that she could shine, earning points to keep her grade average intact, when she turned in her related collage. During the next unit, Melanie gave students six project choices. "Complete two," she said, "at least one must be a writing option." Several chose the oral presentation, but most opted to participate during class or complete an artistic project for their second choice. Melanie felt comfortable about giving choices as she watched the students busily engage in project work. The creativity displayed in the projects made grading more interesting and Melanie heard students talking about their projects in the hall.

Melanie still felt uncomfortable about giving different tests to students. She felt strongly that if she had made accommodations and given choices during the learning cycle, she could expect equal mastery from students. She asked her mentor about tests at lunch that day. "I agree with everyone's needing to show mastery," he agreed, "but there are ways to accommodate different needs. You might ask students to diagram the answer to an essay question or answer some essays in the form of an outline rather than complete paragraphs. The test could ask students to write, draw, and answer objective questions. Students could also be asked to demonstrate competency verbally."

"What about kids who work so slowly they need extra time to finish?" Melanie asked.

"If I write two sections of matching on a test, the slow kids get one. If students have to read a selection and answer questions, these kids get a shorter selection and the same kinds, but fewer questions. Sometimes I even put names on the tests and then I can be assured that the students get different versions of the same test and those with special needs get their personalized tests."

Melanie sighed, "Different versions? I spend hours just writing one test."

"Use the cut and copy tools on your word processor. Put the matching first on one test and last on the second version. Use different cartoons or illustrations on the pages. When they start from different items on the test, they think the tests are entirely different. The switch-around should use only minutes of your writing time."

With these ideas, Melanie went back to her classroom. She was thinking about having students draw and label the parts of an 1890s invention line on the next test.

CHEATING ON TESTS

Cheating is one of those subjects such as abortion: People are rarely neutral about it. You may hear some heated debates in faculty rooms over methods of dealing with cheaters. Your school may have a written policy to cover cheating incidents.

In a world where students hear parents openly discussing ways to beat the IRS or lying to get little Susie or Grandpa into the movies at a reduced price, it's no wonder that students find devious and creative ways to cheat. Cheating techniques have ranged from the wandering eye to the micro sheet rolled in the boot to the full-fledged copying of acquired tests and selling them for profit. Increased Internet access has added another dimension to cheating. Teachers often comment that if students spent as much time studying for a test as they did preparing the cheat sheets, they'd all ace the tests. No one advocates or condones cheating; and when students do cheat, it

Test Cheating

seems to be the teacher's blood pressure that sky-rockets. It is the teacher's day that is ruined. When confronted with their cheating, most students don't feel guilty about material not learned. Nine times out of ten the student is more upset that he or she has been caught.

The key is to set students up for success right from the beginning so they're less likely to cheat. Encourage them to use notes on quizzes, but change quiz questions each period. If they know what you expect, there's less anxiety. Students say they cheat because they are unsure of the material and don't want to risk a low grade because of home or academic pressures. Robert encourages his younger students by telling them they will do better than they think. He tells them to write down what they know.

Unfortunately, some teachers at all levels set students up to fail. These teachers use trick questions or require impossibly detailed diagrams. Tell your students what you expect them to know, why they need to know it, and how they can learn it.

Sometimes, for a test, you might give each student an index card to make into a review tool. Each student compares information with a partner and writes details, formulas, or diagrams on the card. Seeing, writing, and discussing information all reinforce the material. As archaic as it sounds, one of the major aspects of learning is repetition. The more students see the material, write it, talk it, and read it, the more likely they are to remember it. And that, of course, is the goal.

Teach test-taking skills. Show students old tests or give them a practice exam before they take your first graded test.

Some teachers pause at certain points in a test to let students confer for two minutes, and then instruct them to go back to test taking. Unorthodox? Perhaps, but if our ultimate goal is for students to learn the material, what better way than from each other? In many subjects memorization is an appropriate, testable skill. Whatever your philosophy in administering tests, do not lose sight of your curriculum goals.

Even though you try to prevent it, cheating is a fact of life, and students will continue to do it. If a cheating situation occurs in one of your classes, you have several options. Schools vary in their policies dealing with the issue. Check with your administration. Interview other teachers. For most classes, it's an automatic F or zero on the test. Discuss the incident with the student privately. Remind him or her of the consequences for cheating. Call the parents and relate the situation to them exactly as it occurred.

Recently, a student teacher discovered that a young woman who'd been absent was taking a make-up test by copying from another student's test. Obviously, some Good Samaritan had absconded with a copy of the exam and provided it to the making-up student. The student teacher was horrified that a copy had escaped. In a later conference, the student teacher and her cooperating teacher discussed how she could prevent this type of cheating in the future. You can follow the guidelines these two teachers worked out: (1) When passing out tests or other materials that you do not wish to leave the room, make sure you have counted carefully; (2) number your tests or handouts so you know what hasn't been returned; (3) distribute two versions of the test; and (4) circulate around the classroom when administering the tests.

Ultimately, as previously discussed, the best way to keep cheating out of your classroom is to set up your students for success in the first place.

COMPUTER "NETIQUETTE"

As students become more proficient in accessing the World Wide Web both at home and in school, their penchant for mischief increases. Problems arise from the student who steals the mouse roller or switches keys on the board to the student who changes parameters on a computer—thus making it impossible for the next student to complete an assignment. Other students "surf" into inappropriate web sites, plagiarize, send "flaming" (rude and inappropriate) e-mail messages to other students, or even hack into the server that controls the school's computer service.

Many districts are providing teachers with the support of an Acceptable Use Policy for any student or staff member using school computers. This policy might be a multipage document to be signed by both parent/guardian and student, or it might be as brief as a few lines in the student handbook. Either way, students are expected to use computers responsibly. This includes moving away from inappropriate web sites (no filter system can block all the controversial sites from school computers), not deliberately jamming the system, and not writing and/or sending inflammatory material through the system. Savvy teachers are talking daily with colleagues and are developing methods of dealing with computer-based problems and the students who create them.

- Determine whether your school has an Acceptable Use Policy that outlines the guidelines for computer use at your school.

- Find out what the procedure is for students who misuse this policy.
- Before ever allowing students to use the computers in your classroom or taking the whole class to the computer lab, state your expectations for student behavior when using computers.
- When students use the computer lab, assign them a specific computer. Tell them to check their computer when they first sit down and report any broken or missing parts, plugs that have been changed, or parameters that have been changed *before* they begin so that they cannot be blamed or charged for any needed repairs. This teaches them to be observant and proactive about their computer use.
- At the end of the period, have each student turn over his or her mouse so that you can stroll by and do a visual check for rollers before you excuse the class. Remind them that you are protecting them from being wrongly blamed by the next class for missing parts or broken computers.
- If misuse, plagiarism, or vandalism occur, act swiftly and firmly. This is not the time for fifteen gentle reminders. Warn once, then remove computer privileges. If the infraction is severe, report the student to the technology committee or vice-principal during the next break. Because schools invest huge amounts of money in equipment, they will support your efforts to protect the computers and the system.

The best way to avoid problems when students use computers is to plan great lessons. Telling students to click into the Internet and "find something" about your subject area is an invitation for mischief. Your lesson preparation should include time for you to "surf" and identify key sites that contain the kinds of articles you want your students to access. Bookmark these sites or write down the URLs (universal resource locations). Depending on the number of computers you are using, pairs of students or individuals could each look at different sites. You might ask students to not only read and summarize the material at that site, but also evaluate the material: Who wrote this? Is it credible? How do you know this? Does it include "hot buttons" or links to other sites? Does it confirm the information? Using the Internet for teaching should emphasize both gathering new information and evaluating this material for usefulness as well as credibility. Students could then respond by writing in their journals or writing a report, orally to the whole class or to a small group, or by creating a multimedia report on their research topic.

Your media specialist can be invaluable when planning lessons involving computers. There are more and more products (many of us remember them as paper-format research indexes) that are now accessible via the Internet. Students moving directly into the URLs of these products access articles from research journals and daily newspapers. They easily learn to use the help-prompts at the edge of the screen. Soon they prefer this method of research to the less efficient "surfing."

COPIED ASSIGNMENTS AND PLAGIARISM

Sometimes a student will turn in an assignment that is practically identical to another student's work. Invite the two students to comment on the similarities. Usually, one of the students will admit that he or she has copied the work. They realize that you weren't born yesterday and that some coincidences are just too amazing. Depending on the original task, you may wish to let the copier redo the assignment for a late grade, or you may assign a different project that no one else has done. Your plan of action depends on the standards you have set from the beginning.

When Brian discovers two identical assignments, he divides the grade between the two students. He also confers with the students and advises parents of the situation.

On the elementary level, Kathy states that when her students cheat, she expects them to do a different, additional assignment that emphasizes the same skills. Students must do this new work during free time: recess, lunch break, before or after school.

Plagiarism in assignments is something to watch for and in some districts is a major disciplinary infraction. When a student turns in a report on snowboarding copied from the latest kids' sports magazine in lieu of an original story, you must deal with the issue. Many schools have a written policy on plagiarism and the consequences. Define plagiarism for your students, and explain why it is illegal and inappropriate. Teach your students how to give the author credit for copied material. Kathy says, "This author must be given credit for his or her work. You are still responsible for the original assignment. You will need to write your own story."

One way to check for plagiarism is to compare a student's writing style on a prepared-at-home paper with one written in class. If you have suspicions, create an in-class writing assignment. This, along with earlier samples of the suspected plagiarist's work, will give you something to bring to a student conference: Comparisons of sentence structure, usage, general sophistication or style of expression, and level of vocabulary will all provide clues. Plagiarism is a difficult matter, but it can be handled.

At the secondary level, plagiarism is definitely a problem—especially with research projects or book reports. Students have discovered how easy it is to download a complete paper from the Internet. As with elementary students, discuss the gravity of plagiarism. Make sure students know how to cite sources and give practice in writing bibliographies. Often the citation page from a plagiarized paper will not match your style requirements. Provide directions that require original writing as part of the assignment. If students have done career research, have them write about their day on the job ten years from now. Directions that include interviews, connections with personal experience, or opinions involve students directly and reduce plagiarism. Requiring that students turn in a rough draft along with the final copy also helps.

Sometimes you may sense that a piece is plagiarized, but you can't find the original source. When this occurs, question the student and be honest about your doubts. If the student is adamant that the work is original, but your doubts are still strong, you could ask the student to sit in the classroom and write another version of the same material without other resources. Students must understand that the learning of the material is the goal, and that plagiarism undermines that goal.

MISSING ASSIGNMENTS

A retired teacher friend of Barbara's has a favorite saying: "He who deceives me once is a fool; he who deceives me twice is a wise man." Apply this to your students. If a student offers what appears to be a legitimate excuse for not having an assignment, be reasonable. Acknowledge the problem, discuss a fair compromise, and perhaps agree to an extra day to complete the assignment. Remind the student of the consequences should the incident occur again. Facing up to consequences is a lesson in responsibility.

Late Assignments and Make-Up Work

Kathy found herself at the end of each week with a two-inch stack of make-up work in addition to her regular assignments. Her policy had been to allow students to turn in missed or "redo" assignments any time before the last two weeks of any grading period. Her intent was to help ensure success for her students. What she was inadvertently accomplishing instead was overworking herself and enabling her students to put things off or turn in sloppy assignments the first time. During the second semester, Kathy finally realized that this policy was burying her in paper. She knew that change was impossible at this point in the year, but she began to revamp her policy for the following year. A late/make-up policy that might work for you could include these three elements:

1. If a student is in school, the assigned work is due. Have students hand it in at the *beginning* of class so they will not use your class time to complete the previous day's assignments while you are presenting today's lesson.
2. Make-up time is typically two days for every day absent up to five days to complete the work. In special cases, a counselor or administrator may help you set up a contract or independent study for make-up work. Extended absences will be handled according to the circumstances.
3. If you allow students to redo assignments, you may want to establish a strict "work due within the week" policy. This means that an assignment from Tuesday needs to be redone and turned in by Friday.

One of the major annoyances for many teachers is the late assignment. You've already handed out an expectation sheet the first day of class that clearly states how much a student's grade will be reduced based on the number of days an assignment is late. A grade of B, for example, would become a C. Stress to your students, from the beginning, the importance of meeting deadlines. When you enforce deadlines, you help build students' competence. You can always allow some redoing and revising of daily work *after* deadlines are met. Some teachers feel that a student who eventually does an assignment, albeit late, is learning more than the student who does nothing. Encourage students who have missed a deadline to do the assignment anyway, help them to recognize that a late grade is better than no grade.

Absences

Study groups established in the beginning of the year can provide members with information presented in class that a member missed because of absence. This is helpful to you because it alleviates questions that teachers hear at the most inappropriate times: "What did I miss while I was gone?" To help absent students get back up to date when they return to class, you could keep a large calendar in the room listing what you did in class each day. This calendar could also note pending due dates. Absent students could check the calendar to find out what they missed. You might post a make-up date two days after a quiz or test. Allow students a make-up time before or after school. Post a time that is agreeable to you and makes it possible for students to attend. Do not feel that you must skip every lunch and remain in your room every minute for students. Barbara meets with students one lunch period a week for any make-up session. If students choose not to come, they lose the grade.

A question that is sure to grate on your nerves like a fingernail scraped across the chalkboard frequently comes from parents after absences due to illness or before or after extended vacations: "Jenny didn't miss anything, did she?" Using your best social skills and most diplomatic manner, let the parent know that yes, indeed, Jenny missed some things. Explain that while Jenny won't be able to duplicate the learning experiences she missed, you will give her some suitable make-up assignments to help her cover the same material. When you know in advance that a student will be absent for several days or weeks, you can give that student some standard assignments to complete during the absence. Here are some suggestions.

- The student should keep up with any assigned reading done in class.
- The student should spend a minimum of fifteen minutes daily reading self-selected materials.
- The student should complete any daily assignments that can be easily understood. (You shouldn't assign new concepts unless you have talked with the parents and they understand that they are introducing the concept to the student. This will work in some families and cause tension in others. Be sensitive to the situation.) If the absence is for an extended period of time, make a note in your anecdotal records and list what work was completed.
- A student going to Mexico on a two-week vacation will have experiences that cannot be duplicated in class. You might ask traveling students to keep a daily journal of activities on the trip or to select a subject pertaining to the destination and prepare a report to be presented to the rest of the class. A second grader spent the week after the winter holidays in Hawaii and kept a daily journal detailing daily activities. She took photographs, drew pictures, read books on volcanoes, and gave a presentation to the class about the volcanoes on her return. The whole class benefited from that trip.

Help yourself by creating a form to keep track of assignments for ill or traveling students. You or study partners may fill in this form, depending on the age of the student and the type of activities. If a student is able, e-mail or voice mail can be used to communicate with the teacher or study group.

It's difficult when, only minutes before the departure, a parent asks for assignments for two weeks. It is perfectly reasonable for you to explain that it is impossible for you to give advance assignments without several days' warning, but try to prepare something for the student to take along. Then use this opportunity to plan ahead and sketch out your lesson plans for the whole class.

HOMEWORK PROBLEMS

At all grade levels, homework is becoming a major issue. Your district may already have policies regarding homework, or it may not. In any event, you may certainly assign homework. On the other hand, students today have after-school commitments ranging from gymnastics to piano lessons, or they are cared for away from the home until the evening meal. Furthermore, in a recent survey of high school juniors, almost 80 percent had jobs during the school year.

At a recent meeting of educators and businesspeople, this topic of homework versus outside commitments—specifically employment—surfaced. Several teachers at the meeting suggested to the businesspeople that students should not be closing businesses or otherwise working late on school nights. The businesspeople, especially those in the restaurant field, argued that, although they sympathized, their labor needs were best met by willing high school students. A lengthy discussion followed, with no solutions.

These same teachers then addressed groups of parents at a Back-to-School night, sharing concerns about the rapidly growing number of students who dash from the classroom to the job. Many parents agreed that the priority should be academics and that if their Tim or Nancy were slacking off, the job would have to go. In reality, though, the grades often continue to slip and the student remains gainfully employed.

This is not to suggest that students shouldn't work or participate in after-school activities. Life does extend beyond the school day. However, the growing trend of students with many after-school commitments is creating a whole new perspective on homework. Many parents and educators argue that homework, if it is required, should assume top priority; the job or extracurricular activities are secondary. Others don't agree and react to undone homework with a shrug and an "Oh, well." We have found it fascinating and disturbing over the years to witness this evolution.

A colleague tells of a recent conversation with a student:

> "So why do you work?"
> "I have to work to have money for gas and insurance, for my car."
> "So why do you need a car?"
> "So I can get to my job."

This ludicrous logic made perfect sense—to the student. No wonder he had no time for homework!

In the past, students would fabricate hundreds of excuses, be absent, or negotiate for an extra day when an assignment was due. Many students will tell you what Greg, a tall, quiet, droopy-lidded young man, told Betty when she asked him why he didn't have his assignment: "Sorry, Mrs. N, I worked all weekend loading cargo and didn't get my homework done." He yawned. "I need more time." What he needed was sleep. Others will announce that their printer is not working and hand you a disk not compatible with your system. You can't even check to see if the homework was done.

However, even if students aren't rushing off to work or soccer, they may face many evenings without support or encouragement. From kindergarten through high school, teachers have heard students say, often tearfully, that they didn't understand the assignment and no one was home to help. It's difficult to reprimand students for something beyond their control.

The homework issue for you boils down to this: Either the work is turned in, or it isn't. When the work isn't turned in, you might give the student a zero, but that doesn't meet the learning objective. The real problem is that the student without completed homework is not ready for the next day's assignment. If you are an elementary teacher, you could require that the student complete the missing work at school that day. On the secondary level, you could allow more out-of-class work time with a grade reduction, but make it clear to the student that the homework was given to achieve a learning goal and is not busy work, to be done whenever (and if) the student chooses. At any grade level, you might give homework a completion check in your grade book so that the assignment is acknowledged, but you aren't overburdened with grading.

You can use several techniques to ensure that your students understand the homework assignment before they leave the classroom. Students might write down the assignment and share what they wrote with others in their study group. You could also check assignment understanding as a way to close each lesson. As Robert stands at the door to say goodbye to his grade-schoolers, he asks each child to tell him what homework she or he is going to remember to do that evening. In a middle or high school, you might use the last minute or two before the bell to ask, "What's your assignment for tonight?" You could direct this question to the class at large or to individual students.

To hold students accountable for homework involving reading, you may wish to administer a short quiz that specifically tests recall. The responses may simply be a word or phrase, so the quizzes are easy for you to grade. If you teach in a secondary school, alter the questions from period to period to alleviate information exchanges between classes. This is easily done on an overhead or TV monitor.

One of your toughest homework-related calls is that well-meaning parent who does the homework for the child. If a student who normally hands in an assignment that squeaks past failing suddenly turns in work that resembles a doctoral dissertation, you have cause for concern. If the student insists, after a conference, that he or she did do the work, you might verify this with a parent. If the parent also insists that the student did the work, and parents occasionally will, the in-class work should tell the tale. Whatever your decision in such a case, make sure that the method you choose to deal with the student is legal. In other words, the procedure is the same: You acknowledge the work that was done and then you make time during the day for the student to do additional work that demonstrates knowledge of the concept. The student and his or her parents might have done a book report together. During the next day the student might give you an oral report that exhibits an understanding of the book.

EXTRA CREDIT

You will also need to be prepared to answer questions regarding extra credit. Thinking through these points first should help you formulate answers to students' questions:

■ Are you going to allow extra-credit activities to replace required assignments that the student chose not to turn in? Many teachers adopt the philosophy that extra credit is enrichment and should be done only after all required assignments have been completed.
■ Does the extra-credit assignment meet a specific educational goal?
■ Can you make the directions clear enough so that the student can complete the assignment independently?
■ Are you willing to invest the time to evaluate these extra-credit projects?

If you are a beginning teacher, you're already overwhelmed with daily planning and grading. You probably don't have the additional time required to plan and evaluate extra-credit projects. The more experience you've gained teaching, the more likely you are to have developed a file of easily evaluated, educationally valid, extra-credit activities. If you choose not to offer extra credit, your comment to students might be, "I do not accept extra credit because I'm more interested in having you do the best job you can on required work." The final decision regarding extra credit remains your individual choice. The four points just provided should help you make that decision.

CONCLUSION

No matter how students are assigned to classes, their needs will vary. Some may be "at risk" or diagnosed as having a learning barrier. Others bounce from parent to parent like a tennis ball and may not know where they're going to be sleeping that night. In that same class, you'll find motivated and gifted students. So in planning and presenting your lessons, creativity and flexibility are critical. All students need a clear perception of the concepts you covered in class. You can accomplish this by:

- clearly stating the objectives.
- explaining the material's relevance.
- reviewing how and when the learning will be measured.
- leading the students through the material in a series of steps and offering choices to demonstrate learning.

Your students will be learning, and you will have drastically reduced your curriculum-based problems.

Finally, you have to set a fair, consistent policy to deal with cheating, copied or plagiarized work, late or missing assignments, makeup and extra-credit work, and homework.

6

Record Keeping

The best piece of advice
I could give a new teacher is
to be organized! Organization, quite
literally, saved my sanity.

Deborah Watts

The school principal came to Robert needing information on a student's attendance. A local judge had asked how many days the student had been enrolled in the district. The authorities needed the date of entrance, absences, number of tardies, and the date the student checked out. All of this information was in the computer in the office, but the secretary had been sent to the district office with the school's attendance disk, leaving the principal temporarily unable to access this information. Robert's records were the only readily available source. Robert and his principal were able to piece the student's attendance history together within minutes because all the information they needed was in Robert's grade book, on the hard drive on his computer, and on disks.

As you face a new class for the first time, keeping accurate records may be the furthest thing from your mind. There are so many other things to consider. However, you need to establish a plan for keeping track of who attends your class, grades, lessons you've taught, student behavior, and personal records. Your grade book, faculty handbook, and master contract are all legal documents. With a system of record keeping and filing documents that suits your personality and teaching style, you can handle the necessity of keeping records efficiently and leave more time for the other aspects of teaching.

You may come across some wonderful-sounding and elaborate plans for keeping track of daily attendance and grades, but if they don't fit your personality and teaching style, you won't follow through. To help you work out your own system, this chapter outlines what kinds of records you will most likely be expected to keep and offers some examples of ways you can accomplish this record keeping.

ATTENDANCE

Keeping track of attendance and tardies is a daily or hourly chore that you must deal with quickly. Your school will have an established procedure.

Your grade book is the legal record of this information. Whether it's to provide information to an administrator, confer with a parent, fill out a tardy notification, or complete report cards, you need to have easy access to accurate documentation. You'll want to take attendance quickly in the first minutes of class. Having the forms available and your grade book set up are two ways you can simplify and expedite this process

Robert allows a student to fill out the attendance form that must be sent in to his elementary school's office every morning. This job is handled by all the students on a rotating basis. Absences, tardies, and the lunch count are noted, and the slip is then hung on the door to be picked up by an office aide. Robert quickly checks around the room to be sure the report is accurate and then personally marks any absences or tardies in his grade book. When time permits, Robert enters the data into his computer. Robert uses a system of A for absent, T for tardy, and ½ for half days absent. In an elementary classroom, the teacher is responsible for recording attendance only once a day, and Robert's system is not too hard to handle. If a student arrives after being marked absent (A), Robert erases the A and replaces it with a T. Additionally, if a student leaves during the day, Robert notes it with a ½ in the grade book.

Gerry, a high school music teacher, also allows a student to take roll. She feels pushed for rehearsal time and wants to begin class as soon as the bell rings. She assigns a reliable student as secretary to complete the attendance task for her. The student completes the school attendance form and marks an attendance sheet, which is kept separate from Gerry's record of student grades. Later, Gerry transfers the attendance information to her own grade book. Although Gerry starts class as soon as the bell rings and leaves roll taking to a student, she makes mental notes of students who saunter in late or are missing. She is responsible for the accuracy of the records she keeps, and she wants to be on top of the situation; she double-checks the student assistant's record. If you want to try this, get to know your students so you can determine who would be able to handle this task. You could also confer with an experienced teacher in your building about which students would be reliable helpers.

Many administrators, however, do not condone students having roll-taking responsibilities. Betty greets her students as they enter the room and gets them started on the day's assignment, already written on the board. As the students are working, she checks over her seating chart and notes missing or tardy students in her grade book. Betty has six classes each day and sees 160 students. She has devised a system of symbols to denote absences and tardies right in her grade book (see also page 156). Finally, Betty marks those same students

Semester 1		Write #1	Quiz Ch 1	Write #2	Art #1	Unit Test 1	Write #3	Research	Quarter Project
Qtr 1		1-Sep	10-Sep	15-Sep	17-Sep	25-Sep	27-Sep	1-Oct	15-Oct
Period 3	Total Points	50 points	20 points	50 points	30 points	100 points	50 points	50 points	150
	500								
Alex B.	450	48	20	45	37	95	37	48	
Bonnie B.	325								120
Tim D.	200								
Alice D.	490								
SongLei F.	486								
Kathy F.	390								
Heather F.	391								
George G.	300								
Chris G.	452								
Robin H.	497								
Nancy H.	402								
Sunny J.	406								
Juan M.	398								
Fred S.	220								
Amy T.	489								
Maria T.	486								
Laticia T.	453								
Libby W.	397								
Booker W.	498								

absent or tardy on the computerized report sheet that goes to the office.

Betty's principal devised a system for identifying tardy students that most teachers in Betty's school have adopted. A Tardy Sheet is posted by the door with an attached pencil. When a tardy student enters, that student knows to automatically sign his or her name, the date, and the period. Later, Betty has a master sheet where she enters the total number of times that student has been tardy. The sheet allows Betty to proceed with the lesson and holds the student accountable for documenting the tardy, a task that teachers often forget.

GRADES

Planning relevant and creative lessons is the heart of your curriculum, yet monitoring student progress is the blood of this process. You need to allow students plenty of opportunities to display how they are assimilating the content, and you must keep accurate records of student progress.

Kathy was conferencing with a parent who was having some trouble accepting the grade his child had earned in math. Kathy tried to explain to the parent that, while she was not denying that the student could be grasping the concepts covered, the student was not displaying that knowledge. The student's daily work scores were average, many assignments were missing, and test scores were barely passing. Finally, in desperation, Kathy reached for her grade book and said to the parent, "Perhaps we need to look at the grades again. I may have made a mistake." Kathy had recorded daily assignments and test scores, made tally marks noting participation, and kept track of the completion of in-class and homework assignments. By looking at the grade book, the parent began to understand why the child had earned the specific grade.

Recording observations, assignment and test scores, and class participation can be a time-consuming job. Try to find ways of streamlining this tedious task. Numerous computer grade-book programs are readily available. These programs will weigh (value) special assignments and test scores, average grades, and allow you to print out a weekly or midterm grade report. It will take you extra time to become familiar with a computer program and to enter all your students' names into the computer at the beginning of the year or each new term. However, in the long run, using a computer grade book can save you time. Brian enters all of his grades into a computer. He records scores on a daily basis in his grade book, which serves as a backup hard copy. Then, at least once a week, he sits down and updates the computer file. He is surprised at how little time it actually takes to do this. At midterm, Brian prints out class averages, and within minutes he is able to fill out progress reports or provide this information to students, counselors, or parents. Additionally, any time during the year when he has a parent conference, Brian can print out an individual's grades. Brian's software also allows him to show percentages of grades earned in the class.

This system works well for Brian because he's a computer buff. Betty, on the other hand, uses her personal computer for word processing but can't be bothered by the extra time needed to enter students' names and scores into the computer. She keeps track of everything in her grade book and uses a calculator to average grades when needed. Neither Brian nor Betty permits students to record grades in the grade book. Again, the method you choose must fit your personality while also promoting correct results. The key to record keeping is accuracy. All records should be secured, including data files and backup disks.

The most efficient way to set up your grade book is to enter students' names in alphabetical order. Elementary teachers set up separate pages for attendance and each subject taught. Middle school, junior high, and high school teachers have one page for each class period. You could keep attendance on this same sheet or have an extra page for attendance.

As you create assignments, determine how many points a student will receive for completing the task or if you will assign a completion grade. Then, when you grade the assignments, you could record the total points possible at the top of each column and enter each student's score in that column. Noting the assignment at the top or bottom of the column helps you quickly identify needed make-up work or missing assignments. (See the example of Betty's grade-book sheet.)

Robert uses a system of +, /, and – to record completion grades. He does this for homework assignments and daily work completed in class. This not only saves him time correcting work but also makes it easy for him to keep track of students' progress. Then, when it is necessary to average grades, a + is worth three points, a / is worth two points, a – is worth one point, and a zero denotes a missing assignment.

Robert also encourages students to share what they know during in-class discussions. While most school districts discourage teachers from giving grades based on attitude, you can reward students for positive in-class behavior by keeping qualitative participation grades. Betty makes a tally mark by a student's name as each contributes to class discussions. This not only allows Betty to observe and keep track of students who contribute but also allows Betty to note if one student is being given more response opportunities than another. She looks over the log to see if anyone is dominating the conversations while another is being left out. Betty determines how many times she would expect each person to respond. This would indicate the total number of possible participation points and serves as the standard when she averages grades.

LESSON PLANS

Chapter 4 details how to write lesson plans. We mention them here again because they serve as a record of what you have covered in class. If a student, administrator, or parent inquires about content taught during a specific week, paging back in the lesson plan book can provide information your brain cannot recall at that instant. Robert refers to his lesson plan books from previous years to determine if he is pacing himself and will have time to accomplish his learning objectives. He also reads over these plans to review how he taught specific concepts or units of study. Your lesson plan book will serve as the log or journal of your teaching year.

Sometimes you will need to reserve material or equipment in advance. If you've kept a record of when you used materials previously, you can plan your order ahead. Brian has to fill out his video requests in March for the following year. During his first few years of teaching, he was unsure of what was available and how to judge when to order that material. While he doesn't stick to a strict schedule year after year, he does go over last year's plans to get a general idea of when he and his students will be exploring topics. He then orders films to enhance the curriculum.

Mike keeps loads of detailed information in his kindergarten plan book along with lesson plans. This information ranges from his favorite play dough recipe to the name and phone number of the woman from the Poison Control Center who gave the great presentation last year. He refers to last year's plan book to see how many parent helpers he needs to contact for the field trip to the science museum. Mike's plan book is a log, not just of his learning objectives, but also of what his class was able to accomplish, what equipment he'll need for a successful project, and changes he wants to make in the unit the next time he teaches it. He has a record of the sequence of instruction, length of time required, and notes about what went well or flopped.

STUDENT FILES

As you fill out referrals for admission into special programs, receive notes from parents, file a discipline report, or complete a report card, you need to keep a copy. Elementary teachers can set up a separate file for each student. The file then holds all the paperwork and correspondence pertaining to that student. Junior high, middle, and high school teachers cannot logistically set up a file for each student. Betty solves this problem by having one folder for each type of form. She maintains another folder for correspondence. Within each folder, the forms are kept in alphabetical order by student name.

It is essential that you keep track of discipline referrals and attendance. If you ever have a serious problem with a student, your only successful course of action must be supported by the documentation you've kept. Chapter 2 on discipline outlines, in detail, how and what you need to keep track of to ensure due process.

Student files are also the place to record amusing anecdotes and positive things that happen in class. For example, being able to share a student's insight about the difference between engineering and inventing establishes a lasting link between you and a parent. Mike uses a three-ring binder that holds a personal information sheet, previously completed by a parent, on each student. This is followed by a blank sheet on which Mike records classroom observations. He writes down at least one of the positive things that has happened in class that week to each of his kindergarten students. Mike also notes any problems he is having with students. These observations are nonjudgmental and simply record what has occurred. Mike carries the notebook home when he has to make calls to parents in the evening. He then has access to phone numbers and parents' names.

Years ago a colleague of Betty's noted a student's behavior by writing a derogatory comment next to the student's name in the grade book. The grade book mysteriously disappeared. A short time later, the teacher was confronted by the administration. The thief had made sure the contents of the grade book became public knowledge. The parents, angry with the derogatory comment, stormed into the principal's office. This story illustrates why you need to keep your records objective, nonjudgmental, and secure.

One last note about student files. They are confidential records. Observations, referral forms, attendance notices, and personal information are not to be shared with others and should be kept in a locked file. If you are careless with this type of information, you could be exposing yourself to legal action, and you are betraying the trust you have tried so hard to establish with your students.

PERSONAL FILES

Master contracts, faculty handbooks, insurance policies, and faculty bulletins are all legal documents and contain information that you are responsible for adhering to. While you are expected to follow all the rules, regulations, and suggestions, no one can expect you to remember all of this. Save yourself time and frustration by setting up a file for all this information. Whenever you have a question about what you should be doing, you can refer to the handbook or the appropriate faculty bulletin. Brian recently read in his weekly "Notes for Notice," his school's faculty bulletin, that the principal was reminding teachers to stand in the hallway between classes in order to ensure correct behavior and reduce littering. Brian was confused. Based on information in the teachers' handbook, Brian thought he was supposed to be inside his classroom as students entered. By standing in or near his doorway, Brian discovered he could help reinforce correct hallway decorum as directed, yet still greet incoming students and keep track of what was happening inside the room. In this case, the faculty bulletin is considered a legal written document, and Brian needs to observe it as well as directives in the teacher's handbook.

For financial reasons, you'll benefit by keeping records of your personal absences. Tami's paycheck, one month, reflected an amount less than what she expected. She didn't know why she had been docked. When she called the district office to inquire, she found out that the record showed she had been gone for two days that were not allowable sick leave. Since Tami keeps track of signing leave reports, she was able to check with her building secretary the next day and clear up the matter quickly. If Tami hadn't had these records, it would have been difficult to resolve this matter.

You may want to add these items to this file of personal papers: a copy of your signed contract, letters of your assignment, observations and evaluation reports, paycheck stubs, and other communication concerning your employment.

CONCLUSION

Keeping accurate records is one of your duties. It may not be your favorite thing to do, but it is essential. Set up a system that is easy for you to maintain—one you know you are likely to follow. Don't think that just because something works for someone else it is going to work for you. As long as you can locate information and you are accurate, your bases are covered. Keeping records secure is critical. It is prudent to keep a hard copy and to back up electronic data. Things you'll need to keep track of include attendance, grades, what's happened in class, family communications, and personal information.

chapter seven

Liabilities,
Safety, and
the Unexpected

Always remember, you _do_ make a difference.

Janet Cherry

Jeff is a science teacher and a coach. Enthusiastic, sympathetic, and kind, Jeff is a hero. Teachers don't see Jeff much, as he's usually in his room chatting. The students, eager to have finally found an adult who relates to and understands them, will tell you he's their favorite teacher.

Jeff began to receive notes. Unsigned, they were harmless enough, mostly thanking Jeff for being such a caring teacher and for being "so cool." Since Jeff spoke with so many students and the notes were complimentary, he shrugged and forgot about them.

The notes continued, and finally a quiet blonde girl began to seek Jeff out between classes, at lunch, and after school. A caring teacher, Jeff listened as she relayed problems of drug and sexual abuse, divorced parents who shipped her from state to state, and other horror stories. Jeff assisted the girl in obtaining help from counselors, nurses, and school psychologists.

One rainy fall night, Jeff was curled up in front of his fireplace with a bowl of popcorn, enjoying a rare evening of watching football instead of coaching it. His doorbell rang. He answered it. On his porch, drenched and intoxicated, swayed the young blonde student. Since students had visited Jeff's house before, he instinctively opened the door and assisted the now-sick young woman to his rest room, where she promptly threw up and passed out. Jeff cleaned her up, drove her home, and left her in the care of an older sister, the girl's "guardian." Several weeks passed before a distraught principal and district supervisor informed Jeff that they were all about to be sued. For the second time in his life Jeff would be going to court: The first had been for a minor traffic infraction; the second would be to face charges of sexual molestation.

Now, years later, Jeff will tell you that the "stupidest thing" he has done was to open the door that night. He'll tell you that although he still cares about adolescents, he doesn't listen to them like he did before or meet with them alone or at his house; he'll tell you that he doesn't offer them rides when it's snowing or touch them even if it's just a pat on the back. He'll tell you that nothing was more frightening than the year of anticipation before the court appearance. Waking up in the morning to the headlines and facing his students, colleagues, and family were a living hell. Jeff knew he was innocent, but the accusation alone made his life miserable. Such a predicament had never occurred to Jeff. He was a teacher; he'd cared about kids.

Never before have educators been so vulnerable. With increasing attention on child abuse, professionals who deal with young people are continually in the public eye.

This chapter is not intended to cite cases or provide detailed discussion about educational law—space does not permit it and that's not the purpose of this book. Laws pertaining to education are too numerous and vary too much from state to state. Laws exist about issues from student dress to search and seizure. When you have time in the future, you may wish to take a course on educational law. You might ask your building administrator about school law sources. For now, here are some suggestions that may help prevent potential problems.

Because most educators are caring individuals, they sometimes don't stop and anticipate consequences before they act. The elementary teacher who hugs a crying third grader or the physical education teacher who offers a ride home to the boy in her second-period class don't often think that a lawsuit may result. The fabricated or exaggerated report, submitted by an angry student or patron on a witch-hunt, will always be unexpected. Most liability problems could be prevented if educators were aware of their extreme vulnerability and used common sense. Jeff learned this the hard way.

Even though you will probably not have time during the first weeks to read them, there are several district legal sources. You will probably have access to a policy manual for your school district. You also have your district contract and bulletins from your school administrator informing you of policies and requirements within the building. Keep all of these bulletins in one place. These are critical, as they represent written law. If a decision must be made, this written information may be what determines guilt or innocence. Keep in mind that if you choose not to follow the policy, you may have to accept consequences.

PHYSICAL CONTACT

It is a sad commentary on our society that we can no longer touch people without a tinge of fear. It's especially tragic that, with so many children in need of affection and attention, we must hesitate. Although it sounds heartless, be careful when touching kids. If you are a "distance" person, this probably won't be a problem. But if you're one of those altruistic types who can't have a conversation without a hug, tap, or pat, be careful. It's best not to initiate physical contact. Sometimes, especially in elementary grades, students will rush up to embrace you in a moment of grief or joy. Avoid frontal hugs. Robert will give such a child a quick, soft, shoulder squeeze, being careful to maintain distance.

Adolescents are less likely to initiate physical contact; however, there are still students who crave affection and will rush at you when you least expect it. Be aware that others may not perceive these adolescent displays the same way they would in the elementary grades. Maintain your distance. Use a sympathetic ear, a kind voice, and a sense of humor to show your students that you care.

Avoid physical contact when you're angry. For some adults, a first response is to grab a student's arm or shoulder. If a conflict arises, literally distance yourself from the student until you both have cooled down. Having the student wait just outside the door allows you both time to think. You can deal with the student later in the period or after class. If you put the student in the hall, be sure to place the student where you can still keep an eye on him or her.

Chapter 2 discusses student fights. Often just making sure that your presence is known is all it takes. Let the students know through your voice that you are approaching. Remaining calm is important. If you are alone, summon a colleague and building administrator. Usually a ring of onlookers is present; one of those students can be sent. Common sense dictates here. You want to protect yourself yet disengage the fighting students if possible. Rely on the tone of your voice and your presence rather than physical contact.

STUDENTS AND YOUR HOME

If a student visits your home, you must exercise extreme caution. As Jeff will tell you, his lack of awareness almost destroyed his career. Seriously consider the responsibilities involved in having students visit your house.

Joyce has a spring picnic for her sixth graders at her home. The students have signed permission slips from their parents that allow them to visit. Many parents help plan the function, which they also attend, assisting Joyce with the supervision. Parents and students have anticipated this yearly event since Joyce first initiated it.

Marc invites his high school wrestling team to his home for a barbecue at the end of the season. Other teachers and coaches attend and, in his school, it has become a traditional closure to the season.

As positive and well supervised as these activities are, there are still risks involved. The following are tips regarding students visiting your home:

- Never admit a student into your home if you are alone. If he or she is ill or intoxicated, have the student wait outside. Provide a coat or blanket if necessary. Call for help. Contact the parents and your building administrator; if the parents or the building administrator cannot be reached, call 911 or your area's physical emergency number.

■ If a student appears on your doorstep to talk, set up an appointment to see the student the following day at school. If the student claims he or she has been abused, call for professional help. If the student claims that a parent has been the instigator of the abuse, contact the building personnel and your school nurse.

Your decisions about students and home visits depend on your community, your relationship with the parents, and your building policy. Just be aware of the risks involved.

CORPORAL PUNISHMENT

This should not be your responsibility as a teacher. Although they still occur, "swats" are ineffective, with many students perceiving them as a "badge of honor." If a school official chooses to administer corporal punishment, it should never occur without a witness. Even though it may be legal, provided it is carried out within strict guidelines, the enforcer risks being charged with battery, which is a criminal offense.

BEING WHERE YOU'RE SUPPOSED TO BE

You may be found negligent if something happens to a student when you're not in the room or not where you are assigned at a given time. If you must leave the room for any reason—use of the rest room, an emergency phone call, your bra strap breaks, or your fly is open—ask a dependable colleague next door to watch your classes until you return. Even then, you still run the risk of being liable if something occurs while you are gone.

Standing in your doorway during passing periods is effective because you can keep your eyes on behavior both in the halls and in your classroom. Administrators appreciate this vigilance.

PERMISSION SLIPS

This is an issue whenever field trips off school property are planned. As students become more mobile and travel to competitions and for enrichment opportunities, obtaining permission from parents or legal guardians will be required. Do not just assume you can herd a busload of youngsters off to visit the local cheese factory or museum. Find out what you'll need to do about obtaining written permission.

EVALUATION

As we have previously discussed, do not use academic penalties for behavior problems. Nothing turns kids off to writing quicker than the 500-word essay on "Why I Shouldn't Misbehave in Class." Language arts teachers invest a great deal of time making writing a positive experience. Such penalties not only cause students to dislike writing; they rarely solve problems. If you've set up your expectations in the beginning, students will know the consequences.

Since the grade book is a legal record, it is critical not only that you keep thorough, accurate records, but that you are able to justify the grades you assign your students. Grades should be as objective as possible. Teachers are often required to explain grades, especially after report cards are sent home. Make sure that you can justify to an angry parent why Susie received a B instead of an A. Also be sure that your grade book or disk is always secure!

LEGAL OBLIGATIONS ABOUT WHAT STUDENTS TELL YOU

Student writing can yield unexpected information. To build trust, tell students from the beginning that anything they write is between you and them unless the audience is otherwise specified. Usually you should not share an essay without that student's permission. However, make it clear to students that if they write about illegal occurrences or life-threatening instances, you are bound by law to report such things. Tell them you want to protect them from harm.

Mary read an essay about the anticipation and excitement over the weekend's pending beer party. The location was included. Mary suggested that the enthusiastic writer change topics, since she was legally bound to report knowledge of illegal activities to the school resource officer. The junior turned in the paper anyway. The party was raided.

Another time, Mary was shuffling through a mountain of papers that had had names removed during peer evaluations. (Code numbers had helped her put names back on papers.) A poem surfaced, heavy with black images of death and suicide. Even students who responded to the anonymous writer sensed something wrong and suggested that the writer seek help. Mary *ran* for help. Counselors had the student out of class in ten minutes. As it turned out, his home life was very stable and he was only experimenting with the power of words. His writing experiment had been successful. Mary didn't get angry with him. She explained the procedure she follows when a student appears to cry for help and that she reports such information because she cares. Mary asked him for an autographed copy of his first thriller when it made the best-seller list.

Teachers need to report any knowledge they have of illegal activities, possession, abuse, suicide, or neglect. The students don't always want help or intervention, but your responsibility to them and to yourself is to report to a counselor, school resource officer, school nurse, vice-principal, or principal.

REPORTING TEACHERS

This is a touchy one. In most cases, if a teacher is doing something inappropriate, it is most professional to talk to the person privately. For example, Mary's student teacher had given a student a ride home. Mary quickly explained the risks and liabilities involved.

In many states and districts you are legally bound to report suspicion of physical or sexual abuse to appropriate school personnel. Often, this is the school nurse. If it's later revealed that you had knowledge of such information and did not report it, you can be liable for prosecution.

If you have suspicion that a staff member is trafficking illegal substances, you will need to exercise extreme caution. Make sure that what you are reporting is factual and not hearsay. A colleague's career and reputation are at stake. Take your time and watch and listen before you act.

If you are aware of other inappropriate behavior on the part of a teacher, student teacher, or substitute (dating students, for example), you need to talk confidentially to your principal, stating the facts without being judgmental. It is then his or her job to make decisions about the information.

DUE PROCESS

Chapter 2 discussed steps in dealing with discipline problems. If you follow the outlined steps, you are allowing your students due process—the right to be made aware of consequences and the right to be heard. Making arbitrary decisions backs you into a corner and no one is happy with the results. Statements to students like, "Either do this or get out of class" accomplish nothing. This becomes a power struggle. If the student does not cooperate and you follow through with your threat of removing him or her from class, you also remove the student's responsibility to complete the assignment. If you back down from your threat, you lose credibility with everyone. If a student has been denied due process, all parties involved are liable. To avoid these types of confrontations, set up clear expectations and consequences in the beginning.

CURRICULUM CONSIDERATIONS

Nick, a high school band teacher, was asked by his principal to prepare his students for a patriotic program. Nick's religious beliefs conflicted with this curriculum requirement. He consulted his family attorney about this issue. He learned that although he retained his constitutional rights he was bound to follow the prescribed curriculum of the school.

During Gary's first year he was assigned to advise the school newspaper. His senior class editor wanted to run a series on teen sex and pregnancy. Gary hesitated to publish articles on such a sensitive topic. The student editor accused Gary of censorship. Gary went to his principal, and she advised him that she would deny the right to publish these articles that advocated premarital sex. This supported the school law stating that administrators have the right to control the content of school publications. In censorship cases of this type, Gary's principal's actions were based on her legitimate educational concerns. School newspapers are a part of the prescribed curriculum.

Robert prepared a unit on fairy tales. He chose alternate reading selections that would meet the same objectives, knowing that any parent could object to his choices. Regardless of grade level, be aware that parents might challenge content materials. It is advisable to have alternate reading selections for such challenges. If you are unsure of how to deal with a situation, consult with your building administrator.

TIME WITH STUDENTS

Although conferences with students should be held privately and not for the ears of others, it is important that these meetings be held with doors open, especially if the student is a member of the opposite sex. In elementary grades it's equally important that doors be kept open to avoid suspicion. It is paramount to use common sense during time spent with children. Although you have the best of intentions, be aware that your behavior, however innocent, may be misinterpreted. If you anticipate a conference becoming controversial, you could invite a colleague to be present during the conference. This would be a situation where documentation may be helpful.

As a beginning teacher, you may be asked to chaperone dances. This is a way to get to know your students in a different setting, and they appreciate your interest and find your presence amusing. They may ask you to dance. Although most teachers will good-naturedly "shake a leg or two," avoid "slow dancing" with students. High school girls, more often than boys, are quick to approach favorite male teachers in hopes of a sultry clinch. As a male, you can save face and decline without hurt feelings if you summon your sense of humor: "I'd like to, Sally, but that fast one wore me

Time Spent with Students

out" or "I promised my wife all the slow ones," should do the trick. As you read this, you may be thinking this is insane, but saying no to a beautiful seventeen-year-old is a very wise decision. It also may save you from a lawsuit and possibly losing your job.

Most districts have specific "chauffeur policies" regarding school personnel who drive students to activities. Coaches and other teachers often drive vans or busloads of students to and from activities. If you are required to chauffeur students, consult state motor vehicle laws and check your school's policy on insurance and liability. You are at risk if you drive students home. Even with others in the car, you're still liable if the student is under age and the parents decide for any reason to press charges. If you're involved in an accident, the results could be disastrous; if not, you could still run a risk of being accused of battery or sexual or physical abuse. You may be surprised how many people believe the imaginative child and not the adult in these cases.

DRESS

Years ago, students could be asked to leave class for wearing blue jeans or skirts that were too short. Depending on your school, you may not have any latitude in determining what students wear in your classroom. The key to decision making and student attire is this: Does the attire interfere with the teaching/learning process? With the emphasis on antidrug and antialcohol programs and gang activity, some schools and districts have adopted policies forbidding clothing or jewelry advocating drugs, alcohol, or gang activity. To alleviate controversies over clothing choices, many districts are considering school uniforms. Check with your administration and adhere to the policy. It is not your job to monitor the clothing of students; however, enforce your school policy concerning student dress.

CONTRABAND

If you suspect that students are harboring contraband (weapons, alcohol, narcotics, explosives, or pornography), report your suspicions to the resource officer promptly. There are many provisions involving search and seizure that are too numerous to mention in this chapter. Refer your suspicions to qualified personnel.

ENFORCED PATRIOTISM

If a child refuses to take part in a flag ceremony, sing the national anthem, or stand during these ceremonies, do not force him or her. Chances are, he or she will tell you why and choose to either participate or quietly sit.

SPECIAL EDUCATION

Special education teachers operate under specific legal guidelines. If you are a special education teacher, you've probably become acquainted with these in your training. If you are a regular education teacher and you have "special needs" students in your class, check with your building administrator or special education facilitator. The student will have an IEP or 504 plan. You are legally bound to adhere to these plans. Due to the nature of the many forms and documents required in special education, accurate record keeping is mandatory.

COACHING

It is likely that, at one time or another, you will be asked to coach. Coaching offers rewards in that it allows you to see a whole different side to kids; often the ones who do poorly in academics shine when placed on a volleyball court, balance beam, or football field.

In many cases, coaching solicits a high degree of loyalty and, consequently, influence. Don't abuse this power. Your primary goal should involve the welfare of kids. Often, in the frenzy of competition, coaches forget this and the victory supercedes what's good for the individual.

You may be asked to coach a sport you've never played or have only engaged in once or twice. Learn the rules. Your school may have an athletic facilitator or director. Ask questions. Attend meetings. The rules of coaching are much like teaching. Consistency and fairness are the keys. Abide by what policy states.

The very nature of sports implies more risk than the classroom. Be where you are supposed to be. If students are training on weights and you're not in the weight room, you could be liable.

As a coach, you may have to treat injuries. Sprained joints, broken collarbones, and eye injuries are some of the most common. Most personnel who work in situations where injuries are likely are required to attend seminars or courses instructing how to administer first aid. This is an area where you are extremely vulnerable. Do not guess about treating injuries. Be sure you've been properly trained before you administer the treatment. You will have to file an accident report. Be certain to check with your school's policy regarding the treatment of injuries and what you are expected to do in the event that they occur.

EQUIPMENT AND THE CLASSROOM

The weight room, science lab, computer lab, kitchen, theater stage, auto mechanics garage, and classroom all offer potential horseplay dangers. A power drill in the hands of a sixteen-year-old could make Stephen King shudder. Train students in equipment use and safety. Practice that is monitored and guided is critical. More importantly, remain in the room with the students and the equipment. This is a major target for lawsuits. If you are going to be gone, plan lessons that minimize equipment use.

ATTENDANCE

Chapter 6 dealt with the importance of keeping complete and accurate records. This cannot be stated enough! Your grade book or disk is the legal record. In most districts, a computer monitors attendance and tardiness. Keep your own records, too. Many of these systems contain glitches, and it won't be uncommon for an attendance officer or administrator to double-check with you. If the process of detention, expulsion, or loss of credit involves documentation, promptly fill out the forms. The paperwork is all part of what keeps you "legal" and "accountable."

SAFETY ISSUES AND THE UNEXPECTED

Intruders

Never in history have we become so focused on weapons and violence in the schoolhouse. Although such incidents are rare, proactive measures may save the lives of you and your students. In an emergency, common sense should prevail. All your decisions need to focus on safety and protecting the students.

Some schools have colored code cards: A "red" card carried to the office by a neighboring teacher or trustworthy student is an immediate signal that danger is present. Many classrooms can communicate with the main office via intercom or phone. Find out your school's process for obtaining emergency assistance. A few years ago, such precautions were rarely considered. Today, it's critical to anticipate emergencies.

If you are confronted by a threatening individual:

▪ Communicate immediately, if possible, with the office, but *do not leave students alone.*
▪ Remain calm and speak quietly; avoid arguing. Listen to the intruder and paraphrase his or her concerns.

- Attempt to separate the intruder from your students.
- Do not block the intruder's escape route.
- Look at the intruder and memorize physical details so you will be able to give a full description.
- If shooting begins, have students get under their desks or lie, face down, on the floor.
- Student safety is paramount. They will be watching you for guidance. Don't attempt heroics.

Earthquakes

One morning Barbara was taking roll while her students were copying an assignment from their texts. Barbara noticed that her podium was shaking and looked out the window to see power poles swaying like toothpick dancers. She realized that she and her students were experiencing an earthquake. Barbara forced herself to remain calm and quietly explained to the students what was happening. Fortunately, the quake was over in seconds, and other than dealing with an excited group of students, no damage occurred. Had the earthquake been more severe, Barbara would have had students move away from windows, shelves, and heavy objects or furniture. She would have had students crouch under their desks and clasp their hands firmly behind their necks. If the quake occurred when students were outside, Barbara would have had them move away from the building and overhead power lines. She would have her students crouch low to the ground.

Flooding and Severe Weather

There will probably be some prior warning, however short, before flash flooding or severe weather occurs. Follow your school plan. Floods will dictate that students move to upper floors or high ground. Tornadoes or storms should send students into center hallways, away from glass. Take time during the year to practice for emergencies and emphasize that the class must stick together and arrive at a designated destination. Once you and your students are instructed to evacuate to a safe place,

- Take important documents such as grade books and discs.
- Shut off electric appliances.
- Shut windows and doors.
- Account for each of your students when you've reassembled.

Evacuation

One cold, November morning, Angie answered the office phone to hear a menacing voice deliver a bomb threat. The principal took action and evacuated the school. Staff and students shivered in the wind while fire personnel searched the buildings. The process seemed to last forever and the teachers and students were finally moved to a nearby church auditorium. A bomb was never found. Your first priority is the student safety. After that, use common sense and discretion.

The Unexpected

Unexpected interruptions are among the most frustrating parts of teaching. These interruptions vary in importance and continue throughout the school year. They may be call slips from the office. Usually the office will notify you of the urgency of the request. If the call slip states "emergency" or "right away," you simply pass the message to the student and proceed with the lesson. Otherwise, excuse the student at an appropriate time. Sometimes you will be interrupted for administrative business such as money collection, class counts, or maintenance calls. Maintain a sense of humor. Refocus the students. If the interruptions become unreasonable, talk with your administrator.

Most school districts have strict policies regarding interruptions by nonschool personnel. Mike found himself an innocent victim, caught between two parents who were fighting over custody of their child. The parent who did not have custody came to school to remove the child. The situation could have become a legal and catastrophic nightmare. Do not release students unless you have written permission from the office or legal guardian.

Fire Drills

Fire drills may be announced or come as a complete surprise. The alarm will always startle you, but that is to be expected. Before the first day of school, become familiar with your classroom exit route in the event of an emergency. Make a map and place it by your door so that all may see it. Include this in your substitute file. When drills occur and students are evacuated, close the windows, turn off lights, take your grade book or disk, and close the door. You can assign students some of these tasks. Make sure all students are accounted for.

Rest Room Visits, the Nurse's Office, and Illness

You will need to establish a policy for students visiting the rest room and nurse's office. Chapter 3 discussed rest room passes and how to address students who take advantage of rest room privileges. There are, however, unique situations which develop.

If you have a student with bladder control problems, let the child know privately he or she may make rest room trips whenever necessary. Discuss with the parents or nurse the need to have some dry clothes at school to help avoid embarrassment.

Allow students to leave immediately if they have a nosebleed or need to vomit. One day, Kathy was talking with a student. Meanwhile, an obedient, but ill youngster was waving his hand in a violent attempt to let Kathy know he was about to be sick. Before he succeeded in obtaining Kathy's attention, he vomited all over himself and the girl in front of him, much to the chagrin of Kathy and her 28 sixth graders.

Some students believe that the easiest way to escape responsibility is to "feel sick." Honor most of these requests. If time permits, talk with the student to assess the situation. Often a comment such as "Why don't you wait until after the test?" or "The discussion we are having is important" will encourage the student to remain in class. If the student begins to exhibit a pattern of becoming ill at certain times or being absent on test days, see your school nurse immediately and inquire about the student. There may be legitimate health problems; if so, a solution needs to be found. You don't want to be cruel and deny help to an ill student. Just be aware that some young people use illness as a convenient reason for leaving your class.

If any of your students have serious health problems, note this on the permanent health record with a colored flag or marker. It only takes a little time to check your files. This will help you avoid any unpleasant or dangerous situations. Sometimes the school nurse will inform you of students with special health problems. Kidney problems, diabetes, epilepsy, and asthma are examples that require special attention. Remember, however, that this information is confidential.

Especially if you teach elementary school, you may witness and take care of things you never imagined possible when you deal with sick students. Make it a habit to reach for the trash can and your latex gloves when a student grabs his or her stomach and complains. Do not touch any body fluids. The custodians are trained to handle these situations. If the emergency is real, a student's face may flush and be excessively warm or cool to the touch. In this case, rush the student to the office or nurse's room. Depending on what you and your students are doing at the time, you may accompany the suddenly sick youngster or entrust that duty to another student. Advise a neighboring teacher whenever you need to leave the classroom for any reason. You may also have the means to summon someone from the office for help.

You will also have the not-quite-so-sick and the not-sick-at-all students who claim to be suddenly ill. You will soon be able to recognize these categories. Sometimes complaints of aches and pains are signals of other problems, and simply providing some attention will help. Anxiety about not being prepared for class or other daytime dramas can cause students to complain. You will need to determine what you are going to do in each situation. Some students will come to you and mention they are not feeling well when, in fact, they are on the verge of throwing up. Others will offer you a detailed description of their latest hangnail. Each student is unique. A drink of water, trip to the rest room, or quiet reading session in the corner may solve the problem if the student's need was for attention. This also may be a ploy to avoid work. If students persist with complaints and symptoms, contacting parents may be necessary. Tell them you are concerned. They may offer some solutions or insight about what is really bothering their child.

Emergency Illness

Over the years, teachers have survived earthquakes, bomb threats, gas leaks, fights, loose animals, rabid dogs, fires, and other disasters. Ideally, you will want to handle your own classroom problems. Should an emergency occur and you need assistance in a hurry, the following may help. You need to be prepared for emergencies from day one.

If a student has a seizure, fainting spell, or serious accident in class, send a dependable student to the office or summon help immediately. Your student or you need to explain the problem calmly and clearly.

If a student has a seizure, place a soft object under the student's head. Don't attempt to restrain. Move furniture away. Prevent other students from crowding the scene. When the seizure has passed, the student should be assisted to a comfortable place to lie down under a nurse's supervision. The remaining students may have questions. Explain what has happened or obtain answers for their questions. They need to understand that it is possible for anyone to have a seizure and that the person is not to be feared.

CONCLUSION

A phrase that often occurs in court cases and legal disputes regarding education issues is "reasonable and prudent." Paying attention to written policy and using common sense should keep you far away from what Jeff had to experience. Twenty years ago, much of what has been stated in this chapter would have been scoffed at as paranoia. Today, such caution is necessary to keep you in your job and out of court.

As violent or emergency situations in the classroom increase, teachers need to be proactive about such possibilities. Remaining calm and exercising common sense are the best tools in such dire circumstances.

chapter eight

Administrators

My Administrator provides direction for the faculty and students. She consistently applies her expectations within the school, and leads by example.

Brett Teller

Administrators had specific expectations when they hired you. One of the judgments they made was that you had the abilities and skills to fulfill these expectations. Administrators interested in your success should be clear and candid about your responsibilities, whether these are stated in writing or assumed.

LOYALTY

Loyalty ranks high on the administrative wish list. All staff members are expected to be loyal to colleagues, the principal, and the school district. This means that you do not criticize teachers, administrators, or policies to students, parents, or others in the community. If you have a complaint, talk to the person who can effect a change.

If a student complains about another teacher, do not get entangled in the issue, even if you agree. Interject with, "Please don't complain about other teachers to me. Talk to that teacher. If you talk behind your teacher's back, I wonder what you say to others about me." Students then rush to

assure you that they *adore* you and never talk behind your back, but they get the point. Of course,
students will sometimes confide legitimate safety
concerns to you. Your job is then to take appropriate action to protect the student.

It represents disloyalty to the district when
staff members complain to the general public
about inadequate textbooks or poor teaching conditions. You might hear a teacher talking down
another school. Instead of complaints, administrators expect loyal employees to volunteer to join
committees working to improve existing conditions. Administrators also expect employees to
look for the good things that happen even in the
low-achieving schools and to provide the best possible teaching situations for students. In other
words, administrators expect you to work to rem-
edy those situations you have control over and not
complain about the rest.

Teachers complaining and whining in the
lounge seldom effect any change. At Ellen's elementary school the principal announced an extensive series of meetings about curriculum and daily
lesson plans. The complaining was loud and ar-
dent in the lounge. Morale plunged. Faculty attended meetings sullenly. Finally, during a
conversation in the principal's office, Ellen said,
"Mr. Roth, I feel that we work well together and I
trust you completely. I would like to ask you a
question. What specific goal or outcome do you
have in mind for these planning meetings? I'm
feeling anxious because I don't understand the
purpose for them." Mr. Roth explained his reasoning both to Ellen and to the rest of the faculty. He
was seeking complete and ongoing knowledge
about what was happening in the classrooms of his
school. He could then intelligently share information with parents and provide stronger support for
his teachers. When the teachers understood the
reasoning behind the project, the whining ceased
and the work began.

TEACHING COMPETENCY

Administrators expect you to arrive with a knowledge base in your subject area. They expect you to plan lessons that accomplish educational goals, appeal to a variety of learners, and fairly evaluate student progress. You will be expected to follow the adopted curriculum. If you feel the guidelines are restrictive or outdated, join a curriculum-writing committee and participate in revision.

FLEXIBILITY

You'll need to be able to both laugh and cry. You must communicate with students and enjoy the age group you work with. Administrators respect flexibility and the ability to adjust smoothly to surprises.

SCHOOL CLIMATE

Administrators expect teachers, both new and experienced, to contribute actively to the school climate. This contribution includes sharing extra duties, being supportive of all programs, participating in all-school projects and assemblies, and exhibiting a positive attitude. School climate also includes clear and honest communication between teachers and administrators. It includes sharing responsibilities when making decisions that affect the smooth operation of the total school program. School climate also means being cordial with other staff members. A positive school climate provides a place where both teachers and students want to come every day to engage in mutual learning experiences. Whiners and complainers drag others down. Administrators appreciate positive people. Positive attitudes are infectious.

COMMUNITY AWARENESS

Administrators expect their teachers to be sensitive to the community that populates the school.

Is the community conservative, liberal, racially mixed, wealthy, or poor? You need to respond with dignity and compassion to diverse backgrounds. You might build lessons that model tolerance and acceptance of diverse backgrounds.

STUDENT SUPPORT

Administrators expect each staff member to do his or her part to develop a positive support network for the children in the school. Be aware of the resources available to students and how to access them. Appropriate use of library services, counseling, reading or music specialists, or even volunteers can provide a smoothly operating integrated learning climate that is tailored to the individual needs of students.

CLASSROOM MANAGEMENT

Administrators expect all teachers to manage the classroom effectively. You must be willing to take appropriate steps to maintain a learning environment. Administrators also expect you to follow the proper procedures if you must take a management issue beyond your classroom.

EVALUATION

Administrators expect all teachers to be able to take constructive criticism. They expect you to self-evaluate and grow professionally.

OPEN-MINDEDNESS

Administrators expect teachers to be objective and to view all situations and personalities as being part of a learning situation. When learning is viewed as the changes in behavior, then all students, teachers, administrators, and support staff are capable of learning. Don't assume the worst. Keep an open mind.

HEALTH

Administrators expect staff members to maintain personal health—both physical and emotional. Extenuating circumstances occur, however. Children or parents may become ill. Accidents happen. You may suffer from poor health yourself. It's important to communicate about these situations with your administrator. Don't be absent frivolously. Excessive absenteeism creates problems—primarily for students. Using common sense about absences will ensure support when you have legitimate reasons for being gone.

THE ROLE OF THE ADMINISTRATOR

School administrators, like teachers, exhibit a variety of styles while doing their job. Some guide their faculties, others lead. Some administrate from behind a desk; others can be found in classrooms, on the playground, or reading to students in the lunchroom while they eat. Whatever the style, you should be able to expect certain things from your administrators.

Support

You can expect your administrator to provide support tempered with a sense of humor and sensitivity. That person needs to be involved in conferences, deal with extreme discipline problems, and provide materials and assistance to enhance the school climate.

If an irate parent storms into your classroom, you need your administrator to take that person to the office, calm him or her, and set up a conference time to solve the conflict. You should expect your administrator to investigate all sides of the situation.

It is up to the administrator to make sure that the custodial staff, cooks, bus drivers, and other support personnel work to provide a safe, comfortable place for students and teachers. Effective administrating will produce a school day relatively free of interruptions. This administrator should recognize your successes and inform the general public about the good things happening at your school.

Role Model

Ideally, you should be able to consider your building principal as your master teacher and role model. She or he should both supervise and evaluate you. Supervision involves observing and providing suggestions for improving teaching techniques. Evaluation involves written summaries of classroom performance for your permanent records.

Many principals or other administrators love to come into your classroom and participate. Brian's vice-principal occasionally teaches a lesson on archaeology for the sociology students. You could ask your principal to come in with a short piece of writing to share. In an elementary classroom, you might invite your administrator in to listen to students read. Robert's principal reads holiday stories to the classes. There are lots of creative ways to get administrators into your classroom to share in the learning process. It is good for your students to see their administrators in these roles, and it keeps that administrator aware of the good things happening in your classroom.

Involvement

You can expect your administrator to be involved in the total school program and understand the scope and sequence of your subject or grade level relative to the total educational program in the district.

Professionalism

You can expect your administrator to demonstrate a positive professional attitude. This administrator should be able to make decisions and follow through, yet be able to admit mistakes and be willing to change.

Evaluations

Most schools have a regular schedule of formal evaluations. When you are evaluated, you can expect to be shown a written copy of that evaluation to sign before it is put in your personnel file. You should also receive a copy for your own files. Read the evaluation carefully before signing it. If you feel the evaluation misrepresents a situation, you have the right not to sign it. The administrator might then adjust the evaluation to your mutual satisfaction. Sometimes this is accomplished through additional observations. If something appears on an evaluation that you do not like, you need to explain your viewpoint clearly and calmly. Usually, the evaluator simply misinterpreted a class event and the misunderstanding is cleared. If the evaluation is not changed to your satisfaction, you are allowed to include a written explanation. Your professional association can advise you if such an uncomfortable situation arises.

If you feel that an administrator is harassing you, you need to begin documenting each incident carefully and seek the advice of your association representative.

ADMINISTRATIVE STYLES

Just as students in your room have different learning styles, administrators have different leadership styles. A principal should know about the different styles and be able to capitalize on the best of those differences. Administrators, like teachers, will exhibit a variety of leadership styles. Some are eager to try change; others feel more comfortable with traditional methodology. If you are uncomfortable working with an administrator, try to work out your differences. Give your working relationship some time. If, however, you find yourself in a situation where you are not comfortable making the expected changes, it may be best for you to stick it out for the remainder of the school term, then try to obtain a transfer. Talk to other teachers and observe in other buildings to try to find an administrator and teaching team that better fits your philosophy and style.

DEALING WITH PRINCIPALS

How you deal with your principal depends a lot on your teaching situation. If you are on a huge faculty, your meetings will probably be infrequent. Communication might be initiated through notes, e-mail, or formal appointments. If you teach on a very small faculty and the principal also teaches part-time, your relationship will probably be more collegial. If the principal was a personal friend before you were hired, realize that your professional relationship will be different from the informality of your friendship out of school.

You can establish effective communication with your administrators before you need their help in a specific situation by inviting them into your classroom to see a special presentation or display. This way, the administrators will be aware of your successes and be more willing to help in the future.

If you are feeling frustrated by an administrative action or inaction, evaluate the situation before complaining. Does the principal have control over this situation? Do you understand the reasoning behind the policy that is driving you crazy? Then, if you want something changed, rather than complaining about it, think about how the problem might be solved, consider who can make the change, and consider how to communicate your concerns and suggestions in a positive tone. Be prepared to live with the outcome.

SCHOOL REFORM

Frequently, schools are under pressure to change in order to meet the competition of the global society. The media compares America with schools in other countries. It compares test scores between schools in a district and is often critical of results. Parents demand the best education for their children; researchers analyze methods and identify trends. These are times of change in education.

Reforms can begin with an idea from a teacher. When a whole staff researches the pros and cons of a change, there is a high probability for success. Gerry's faculty spent three years researching block scheduling. Gerry joined the research committee because she heard that music programs tended to suffer under a block design. Her visits to other schools confirmed her fears and she was able to talk about her anxieties at her school's faculty meetings. She discussed evidence from other music teachers of weakened programs. Eventually, the staff voted by a slim majority to try block scheduling. That fall, their new principal also doubted the concept of block scheduling. He said he would listen to the faculty that year and study their research before changing the class schedule. By the end of the year, the faculty had created a modified block schedule. Suddenly Gerry could see possibilities: She could present more community concerts during the holidays without having students miss other classes. She could hold two-hour dress rehearsals before concerts. That next year, Gerry, her principal, and most of her colleagues taught in a block schedule successfully.

Site-based management is a style of reform used by many school districts. Some central offices turn all decisions for a particular school over to a committee. This committee, made up of teachers, patrons, and administrators, is responsible for budget decisions and school-specific decisions. There can be some positive things happening in a school where the committee makes decisions focused on what is best for students, but negative scenarios can also arise when a teacher is forced to vote for budget cutbacks that affect a particular program and colleague in that building. Committee members might be asked to decide between purchasing enough paper for the school year or ordering new books for the library. Other site-based committees might focus on a single goal for that school such as raising standardized math scores, improving school climate, or emphasizing the school-to-work connections for students.

The "school within a school" concept was developed to give students a sense of belonging when attending a large school. Students are grouped heterogeneously and share a majority of classes during the day. In some designs, one of their instructors is the designated homeroom teacher with related responsibilities. The intent is for the students to work and play together, competing in intramural competitions and achieving successes together. Teachers who share the same group plan integrated curriculum projects, team-teach specific units, and discuss consistent strategies for dealing with students.

"Outsourcing" is the term used when services needed by a school are contracted out to private businesses. Food service might be delivered by a local franchise of a well-known food chain. Private companies could be contracted to complete janitorial tasks. Large companies can provide book processing for libraries. A moving company might be hired to move a school to a new facility. The object is to provide these services at a savings of money or time for the district. The success of each venture depends on the contract between the parties and the integrity of both.

The charter school is one of the newest trends in education. State legislatures are establishing legislative parameters for their implementation. Educators and patrons design charter schools. They differ in structure and function from the public schools. Enrollment is open to all students, and the focus is on what the committee established as the educational priority.

CONCLUSION

When you are hired to teach, you may have an idea as to the school's philosophy. Your school might be the most ethnically diverse in the city. It might be the richest or the poorest. Whatever the "specialty" of your school, when you are asked to join that staff, you are also asked to support that philosophy. If you find that you do not fit in and are uncomfortable, you might consider asking for a transfer for the following year. In the meantime, do your job as professionally as possible.

Most of the time the administrator's expectations of you will be clear. Loyalty is of paramount importance. You need to be loyal in your communications with others and in your behavior. Complete reports, attend meetings, and cooperate with your administrator. If you miss a meeting or deadline—and you will—you will survive. Apologize, do what you need to do to catch up, and get on with your teaching. In turn, you should expect loyalty from your administrators. This mutual support and communication will help to create a climate of positive learning in your school even as it changes and evolves while responding to school reform issues.

chapter nine

Ancillary
Personnel

Be prepared for the wide range
of diversity in the classroom in
terms of academic ability.

If you have an assistant in the
classroom, find things for that
person to do in terms of helping
as many students as possible.

Relax and enjoy - the year goes
by _fast_ !

Joanne Collins

Dorothy King

Cultivate a good relationship
with your specialists (S/LP, PE,
music). Their advice is invaluable.

The support staff in a school includes all adults, both certified and classified, who often are not involved in teaching, yet provide support services that complete the educational plan of the school. Angie, the secretary at Robert's elementary school, is a combination of Mother Teresa and Bill Gates. She bandages knees, patches egos, soothes even the most savage parents, and retrieves lost computer files. The teachers and administrators have changed in Robert's school over the years, but Angie has remained and provided emotional and professional support for teachers, principals, children, and parents.

Support staff members come with friendly, grumpy, hostile, cheerful, overbearing, energetic, lazy, supportive, resourceful, and unhappy personalities. When you work with a support person whose personality doesn't match yours, sparks can fly, and utilizing this person's skills could become awkward for you and your classes. You can't do much to change the personality and moods of this person. It is up to you to get along with this staff member.

Here are some tips for dealing with support staff and ancillary personnel:

1. Introduce yourself and ask about their responsibilities. Ask what services they provide.
2. Be friendly and interested. Don't *tell* these people what you want—inquire if it is possible.
3. If these people meet with classes or individual students during the week, obtain copies of their schedules and keep them in a folder in your desk for quick reference.
4. Discover what you can do for these people to help them do their jobs.
5. Ask how to notify them in case of problems, schedule changes, or needed repairs. For example, when Robert and Ellen exchange library time, one or both notify the librarian of the switch and check to see if the change is

amenable. If applicable, ask how these people can be reached in an emergency.

6. Take time to build and cultivate friendships with ancillary personnel. They are often people with hidden talents and interests that can be shared in the classroom or simply be the basis of rewarding friendships.

SECRETARIES

These people are the heartbeat of the school. Watch them work at a peak time some day and admire their finesse in juggling ringing phones, managing student aides, answering parent questions, passing messages to teachers, applying bandages, and keyboarding simultaneously. Cultivate good relations with them and be unfailingly courteous. If they ask you for a report, they probably needed it yesterday. If you have been friendly and polite, you will be able to ask for an occasional favor and will receive it. Teachers who are irritable toward the secretarial staff don't receive extra favors.

The head secretary is the support person for an administrator, while managing a busy, chaotic office at the same time. Some schools have a teachers' secretary whose main job is to duplicate bulletins, classroom sets of assignments, and transparencies. The teachers' secretary might also be responsible for such tasks as managing the mailroom, answering the phone, and calling substitute teachers. When you ask this person to complete a copy job for you, give clear, readable written instructions and plenty of time to get the job done. Do not assume the secretary will do your typing for you. Occasionally, you might be able to ask the faculty secretary to type a college recommendation on school letterhead if he or she has time. When a secretary does type for you, turn in your rough draft in grammatically correct, legible form. Proofread the finished product. The letter will be sent out with your name, and any errors reflect first on you, then on the rest of your faculty.

CUSTODIANS

These men and women often determine the success of your day. These are the people who have the tools to adjust your stubborn heater, the ladders to help you hang plants, and the brackets to attach your TV monitor to the wall. They empty your trash and clean your boards. Make a point to know the names of your custodians and compliment good work. Expect your students to pick up their own paper snippits—custodians are there for building maintenance, not maid service. If you are doing a cut-and-paste project, stop for a "Snippit-Pick-It" five minutes before the bell, when everyone cleans. Never use cleaning for punishment unless it is a logical consequence for what the child did.

Find out what maintenance is done to your room on a regular basis. If your boards are washed nightly, clearly mark material you do not want erased and expect that once in a while mistakes will occur and you will have to rewrite material on the board in the morning. If they occasionally do a less-than-perfect job, there is often a good reason. If the work is consistently left undone, drop a courteous note to the head custodian.

Different departments do different kinds of repairs, and paperwork must filter through the system before any action takes place. If nothing happens in a week or two, inquire. Sometimes you will get frustrated and do the repair yourself, but this might offend custodians if it appears you are implying they aren't doing their jobs. Do-it-yourself repairs might also create code violations or negate warranties, so try to work with your building custodians.

Repairs are often done during the school day. Paint crews may walk into your class on Tuesday and announce they are ready to paint; your class will need to meet elsewhere for a week. One hot, door-open day, a crew began drilling on the lockers in Betty's hallway. Complaining doesn't make such crews go away, and they can't see dirty looks. Getting angry only frustrates you and models ineffectual anger for the students. Laugh and throw up your hands—not showing the frustration inside—and adjust the lesson. You might have small group discussions with students about heavy equipment or how to deal constructively with inconvenience. Send a student to see if a certain room is unlocked and inquire if that teacher will let you "rent" during the remodeling. Show the students that when these annoyances occur, you need to think of viable solutions and then solve your problem. This is a good lesson in itself.

These same people who sweep and dust often have talents and skills to share with students. The custodian in Angie's school is well versed in mountain lore and helps stage a yearly rendezvous, to the students' delight. Another, now retired, wrote and directed the students in a yearly pageant, one highlight of that small community's holiday celebrations.

LIBRARIANS/MEDIA SPECIALISTS

Depending on your state regulations, most librarians or media specialists are trained as educators with a teaching license and course work in managing media. Many begin with a subject area emphasis, gain teaching experience, then work for media certification. Their primary job is to manage library staff, the media collection, the associated hardware, and the media budget. One thing that is consistent among all librarians or media specialists is that each is concerned with doing a professional job. As information in our society increases at its current rapid rate, the place of the media specialist will become increasingly important. Students need access to current information, and access to that information through the library is the key. In the future, people with power won't necessarily know more than anyone else, but they will know how to access that information. The media specialist's responsibility is to support the curriculum and reinforce research skills for both students and staff members.

The types and personalities of media specialists are as varied as those of any other staff member in your building. Some guard their collections and view each book stolen as a personal attack. Others look at their job as an escape from the classroom. Some can become an integral part of the school, arriving in classes with books, teaching minilessons in research techniques, and beating the corporate bushes for donations.

The role of a media specialist is currently changing. To different degrees, media centers are utilizing on-line research services, CD-ROM search tools, the Internet, and tool software. Librarians have different knowledge bases and skill levels. Depending on what is available in your media center, you can integrate electronic media sources into your library lessons. A good lesson should balance access to both print and electronic sources so that students have experiences with both types of media. A balance between print and electronic media also helps you cope with the inevitability of electronic failure at some point in your unit.

Utilizing your school's media center can provide support and enrichment for your teaching and give your students practice in using research and library skills. Make an effort to learn about offered services and solicit advice on integrating those services into your lessons. Here are some tips for using your media center effectively.

Get acquainted with the media center well before your class uses it for the first time. Spend occasional prep time in the library correcting assignments, reading the paper, or browsing through the collection. Attend any orientation sessions your librarian may schedule, or, if none are planned, ask for a personal tour. Ask, "What would you like me to know so that I can use the media center effectively?"

- Know the procedures: How do you schedule your class into the library for instruction time?
- What is the checkout procedure for books, media, and equipment for teachers? Is needed equipment delivered to the classrooms? What is the general procedure for students?
- When you schedule your class for a library lesson, tell the librarian exactly what the assignment is, providing a brief lesson plan and any student handouts if possible. Tell the librarian what your student expectations are, and what he or she can do to support you.
- Before your class first goes to the library, take time to work through the assignment yourself to make sure the collection will have enough information for all students to use successfully. On the day before going to the library, explain the overall assignment and give students clear behavioral expectations. Make contingency plans for completing the same lesson in the event that the electronic sources fail during your visit.

Don't ever:

- Schedule a class into the library when you know you are going to be absent unless you have cleared it both with the librarian and the substitute.
- Send students to the library to sit and write an essay as a discipline measure.
- Send more than a few students to the library to work independently. If you send more than five, you need to be with them.
- Send students to the library because they have nothing meaningful to do in your class.
- Speak ill of the media specialist—he or she is a professional colleague.

Know what is *not* the media specialist's job:

■ They are not responsible for your class discipline when your students are in the library.
■ They are not usually too happy to run to your classroom to replace a printer cartridge or figure out why your mouse isn't working. It is your job to make sure the equipment is working before class begins and your job to know how to do simple trouble-shooting on your computer. It is not a good idea to allow a well-meaning student to fix the broken object. If their efforts compound the problem, warranties often are negated in the process.

PSYCHOLOGISTS, SOCIAL WORKERS, AND COUNSELORS

If you don't find out during the fall orientation, inquire if your school has the services of a psychologist or a social worker. Ask if these people are in the building every day or on specific days. Introduce yourself, asking about the range of services offered to students. Ask what procedure you need to follow to get help for a student and how to get emergency assistance in a crisis.

Maintaining a friendship with these people can be enlightening. These professionals often have a different perspective of a situation that helps you better understand what a student is doing in your classroom that might be driving you up a wall. These people know if a child has been tested for learning problems and can interpret the results for you. They attend staff meetings and may have met the parents or visited the home. The information they share with you can help you understand the learning patterns exhibited by the child and plan a successful learning situation.

Sometimes you can lure psychologists, social workers, or counselors into your classroom to help you teach. A social worker who wanted to try some techniques to raise student self-concepts in middle school classrooms joined forces with a teacher and a principal. Each believed in the value of a positive self-image in the learning process. Their work resulted in the book *Building a Positive Self-Concept* (by Turk, Horn, and Jacobs, and published by J. Weston Walch). This book contains practical lessons that you can easily implement in your own classroom.

Other topics a social worker or psychologist could discuss with your class could include teen suicide, death, or dealing with difficult people.

These professionals also form student support groups within the school for anger management, substance abuse, teen parenting, divorce, and other topics important to the school community. These groups often meet during class time, and most facilitators try to vary the meeting times, but even though it is frustrating to have these students miss more of your class, remember that this group is often a lifeline for these students. If you are aware of these support groups and know of a student who might benefit from membership, give the student's name to the adult in charge. It is not your responsibility to attend or run these groups unless your training and background specifically qualify you to do so and the administration asks you to sponsor such groups. What is said in these groups is confidential.

Often the psychologist, social worker, or counselor can provide insight about a student who is returning to your class after suffering a personal crisis. Ask what you should say to the class before the student returns and how you should act and respond when he or she is back in class. Classmates need to think about what to say and what not to say. Often these professionals will come to your classroom to prepare students, answer questions, and rehearse appropriate responses. If possible, get these professionals to make contact with the student before he or she returns to classes. Ask how you can be most supportive.

It is risky to provide these kinds of services for a student yourself. It is not a good idea to get deeply involved with students' personal lives. Students can sometimes manipulate you into commitments you are uncomfortable with. Although Mary does not get especially chummy with her reading students, she always remembers the day that Bruce, in all seriousness, asked if he could move in with her. His mother had moved away and his father didn't want him. Her heart broke, but the answer was no. Instead, she talked to the school social worker, who investigated the family situation.

These professionals are our legal protection from lawsuits. Refer any student problems to those specifically trained and authorized to deal with them.

School by school, month by month, counselors have different jobs. Universally, they seem to be overworked and caught in the multifaceted tug-of-war among the needs of students, teachers, administrators, and parents. Some may be assigned to several schools. Some might see just juniors. Each secondary counselor is probably in charge of scheduling students, solving conflicts, keeping track of student credits, and coordinating standardized testing. Counselors also place students with special needs, facilitate conferences, and accomplish a myriad of other tasks. Seldom do they have undivided time to sit down, listen, and counsel their charges. Sometimes you'll feel frustrated by counselors because they are usually busy when you need information on a student. At other times, you'll be grateful for their existence when they plan and run a productive meeting. Counselors can often make quick calls home to check on a sick student when you are in class, and frequently they are the people who gather assignments from six or eight teachers for homebound students.

When you discover a student threatening a suicide or obviously crying for help through actions, words, or writing, go to the school counselor. Inform the psychologist or social worker, too, but definitely tell the counselor. Which person makes the student contact then might depend on who knows that student and the home situation best. This is not your responsibility. Your responsibility is to report.

In less critical situations, counselors can lend you an ear and offer suggestions on how to handle difficult or troubled students. Elementary school counselors often present lessons in class about misbehavior or managing anger. Counselors on all levels are trained to offer grief counseling, and they, in turn, will tell you how to respond as needed.

SECURITY PERSONNEL

Many urban schools employ security personnel. These people have been hired to supervise school parking areas, ensure that people who do not have school business are not in the building, and write incident reports as necessary. In some buildings these people check the identification of every person who enters. Their jobs might involve challenging those they don't recognize and hurrying tardy students to classes. They work to prevent vandalism and with the police department to provide a safe learning environment.

RESOURCE OFFICERS

The schools in some districts have school resource officers. These men and women are trained officers from the police department whose primary assignment is a specific school. They maintain an office in the school and deal with everyday problems from locker thefts and car accidents to substance abuse and truancies. They are also informed if students are involved in crime outside the school realm. On the positive side, resource officers chaperone school activities and speak to classes on student rights. They maintain high visibility to provide a friend and confidant for troubled students.

Students may relate to their resource officer because this adult is not a teacher and not part of the school establishment. This adult is a trained police officer who can advise the students about legal problems, be an advocate, and model the function of a police officer. One year at a large city high school the resource officer was one of the volunteer targets for a pie-throwing booth at the school carnival. He also arranged for a car that had been involved in an alcohol-related accident to be placed in front of the school as a graphic example of the dangers of drinking and driving.

HEALTH PROFESSIONALS

As in the case of most other ancillary personnel mentioned in this chapter, the schedule and job responsibilities of school health professionals are as varied as the number of schools that employ nurses. There are never enough nurses in our schools, and some schools are also using health technicians. The needs of society have radically changed the role of the school health care provider. In past decades, the school nurse's responsibilities included keeping immunization files updated, cleaning skinned knees, screening vision and hearing problems, and sometimes dispensing a few aspirin tablets or cough drops. The image has changed!

School nurses today cannot dispense any medications without written parental permission. These staff members deal with lots of sick students, but may invest much more time counseling pregnant teens, advising students who are suffering personal crises, and intervening between troubled students and their parents. These same health care providers often manage several of the support groups functioning in a school.

Find out the procedure for sending a sick student to the nurse's office. The nurse will usually (but not always) know which students have chronic medical problems. Unfortunately, you do not always get that information. Sometimes the student or the parents do not want anyone to know about the problem for fear the student will be treated "differently." It is frustrating to find out midterm that the student in the back corner of the room is nearly deaf in his left ear. It is frightening to find out in April that a very quiet, low-achieving student is heavily medicated for epilepsy and is having trouble regulating the medication.

You need to know how to recognize a child going into diabetic shock and what to do about it. You need to have current information on AIDS. You also need to notice when a child is squinting, continually missing spoken directions, or acting excessively drowsy in class. In these cases, ask the nurse to call home and check on the situation. Sometimes you might call home yourself and state that you have tried to help the student achieve success in class but are stymied. Are the parents aware of any social or medical problems that might be blocking the learning? If you learn of a medical problem from the parents, you need to then tell the nurse and let him or her interview the student.

Your school health provider will probably make the following suggestions to you:

1. Trust your intuition on whether you feel a student is actually in need of a visit to the nurse.
2. Keep students accountable when they ask for passes to the nurse. Follow up at the earliest possible moment or require that your hall pass be returned.
3. Keep tissues, small bandages, and latex gloves in your classroom. Don't dispense any aspirin, pain relievers, cough drops, antacids, or other medications
4. Don't touch any bodily fluids from students.

Once you know your school nurse and the services offered, you will be able to get information that will help you build the most conducive learning situation for each of your students

INSTRUCTIONAL ASSISTANTS

Instructional assistants, formerly referred to as teacher's aides, are usually noncertified adults who are paid to assist students during the educational process. Their role is to help one or more students achieve the goals stated on the student's IEP (Individual Educational Plan) or to provide full-time support to a single, special needs student. The assistants work under the teacher's supervision and with the teacher's support. Assistants may not legally substitute for or replace that professional. Instructional assistants can be valuable assets when given clear expectations and tasks.

An assistant might be assigned when one or more special needs students are enrolled in a class. This assignment might be based on state and district guidelines, the number of assistants available, or the nature of the students' needs. In a secondary setting, an assistant may help in a class such as biology if several special needs students are enrolled in that section. An assistant might be working in your classroom with a single child who is legally blind or deaf. In a special needs classroom the law mandates hiring assistants. An instructional assistant's job centers on supporting students.

Classroom Teachers and Instructional Assistants

Melanie was arranging her classroom, thrilled to have her first teaching position. A colleague introduced himself as the special education teacher in that building. "I wanted to talk to you about some of my students who will be in your history class," he said, ". . . about their learning needs plus give you the good news that the district has hired an assistant to help these kids during your third-period class." Melanie was skeptical about having another adult in the room watching her teach. She asked what was expected of an assistant. "Well," he laughed, "no paper grading or anything like that. Just use him as you see fit to help the students. Do take time, however, to discuss confidentiality and exactly what it means. Aaron's a young man who has a community education degree and a ton of enthusiasm."

Melanie spent time that evening reading the journal she had kept during student teaching. She noted she had written about wanting more time to help students and brainstormed a list of ways this assistant might help. She also read the district special education manual she received at the new teachers' meetings. Melanie envisioned an assistant who moved through the room, helping everyone. She decided to make a list of classroom expectations for her assistant.

When Melanie met Aaron the next day, she told him what she hoped they would be able to accomplish together. "I need you in class before the bell rings, of course, helping your students get ready to work." She continued by saying that she thought he would be most useful in the beginning by pulling a chair between the desks of his four students and taking notes on her class presentation while monitoring the note taking of the four. "Tell them that as long as they make an effort, they will be able to use your notes during study time to complete their own notes and assignments, or to review for a test. As they become more independent and I change seat assignments for everyone, you could move to the back and keep an eye open. If you see any student struggling, you could quietly give some help."

Other students began to watch Aaron to see what he thought was important to put into his notes. He, in turn, was always willing to share his notes with any student. Soon Aaron was moving throughout the room, coaching and helping. That technique was effective during collaborative group work, too. Aaron first began working with the special needs students and then began working with other groups, sitting where he could keep an eye on his newly independent charges.

Melanie suggested that Aaron discuss signals with his charges. If one of his students felt overwhelmed in class and about to lose control, the signal could be flashed and Aaron would help that student leave the classroom quietly. A signal could be as simple as pulling at the right ear and catching the assistant's attention. Melanie explained that she expected Aaron to be proactive. She expected him to support and enforce the classroom rules and to be aware of the interaction in the classroom. She expected Aaron to react to any student conflicts occurring out of her hearing. They role-played some of the kinds of things Aaron might say in these situations.

Melanie and Aaron talked about ways to help students respond without "feeding" them the answers and how to avoid embarrassing a student. In October, Aaron asked how he might help an extremely shy student respond aloud during a discussion. They planned several approaches. During the year, Melanie and Aaron developed a sense of teamwork.

For unit tests, Melanie asked Aaron to take his four charges out into the hall and simply read the test aloud. He was to offer no other help. Before the second test was administered, three other students who got nervous taking tests asked to join Aaron's group.

Melanie was fortunate. She was assigned an instructional assistant who was competent and cooperative. She had a clear sense of what she hoped to accomplish using her assistant. You may not find yourself in such a situation. The assistant who is assigned to you may already have an idea of what the job is and may not be open to suggestions.

Special Education Teachers and the Instructional Assistant

In another school in that district, a newly hired special education teacher faced the opposite situation. When hired, she was told she would be working with two wonderful assistants: one who had been in the high school program for eleven years and who had now transferred to middle school, and another assistant who had been with the same handicapped student for three years. Instead of being the supportive colleagues this new teacher expected, the assistants often created problems of their own. The one-on-one assistant cuddled her twelve-year-old charge in spite of both parental and teacher requests to the contrary. The special education teacher had several uncomfortable encounters with this assistant until she "got her way" and the assistant started teaching the boy that handshaking was a more appropriate behavior at his age.

The second experienced assistant also proved difficult. Although she did provide a lot of the district-specific knowledge that the special education teacher needed, she also did things "the way we've always done them." The special education teacher could not get this assistant to mix into the class, supervising the special needs students and helping anyone who needed it. The assistant would move to the back of the room and wait until her charges came to her. One day she watched one of her students burst into tears and shout a familiar four-letter expletive. The assistant did not act until the classroom teacher asked her to remove the student. "She's got to learn to control her mouth now. They'll never stand for that kind of behavior in high school," was the assistant's comment during the conference with the vice-principal, the special education teacher, and the student. The student looked simultaneously bewildered, angry, and frustrated.

The special education teacher also felt frustrated. She had made clear statements to her assistants about what she needed them to do, but they usually did what they felt was right. The teacher realized that because her time was devoted to other students, she had no way of monitoring what assistants did in the classroom with their charges. The year dragged on with little improvement. Finally, after the two assistants complained about work evaluations that were less than stellar and included specific improvements that needed to be made, the special education teacher went to her principal for advice. "You did everything right," the principal counseled. "I liked how you wrote their evaluations with specific things to improve—just like you write your IEPs. You also have to realize that your assistants can never be your friends and colleagues. You are their boss. They don't have to like it, but they do have to follow your expectations or try another job. And sometimes, in a situation like this, you just have to survive the year, and you and I will look at the staffing situation this summer."

Assistants in the classroom are seldom perfect and they are seldom awful. They, too, have good days and bad. Most are there because they have a genuine affection for kids and most will accept your training advice. Establishing your credibility with assistants and classroom teachers will seem daunting on the first day of school, but always bear in mind that you were chosen for this position because your interviewers had confidence in you and your training.

VOLUNTEERS

Volunteers, like all other people in the school structure, come from diverse backgrounds. Some volunteer on a regular basis, others arrive as guest speakers, in-room helpers, computer support people, or presenters of special teaching units. Some colleges and universities are now requiring community service as a graduation requirement. Recently two senior engineering students planned, designed, and manufactured huge examples of simple machines for third grade math students at Robert's school. Preservice education students planned minilessons to introduce each concept. The final outcome lesson brought all six machines and university students into a classroom filled with wildly enthusiastic children. The tiniest girl was able to lift her biggest classmate with a finger on the lever machine. Down the hall in a fifth grade classroom, horticulture students from the university were talking to students about what plants would go into a butterfly garden they would plan together in the city park the next spring.

Take note of how other teachers utilize volunteers. If you feel a volunteer would enhance your program and you have a clear idea of the specific jobs you would like your volunteer to accomplish, contact either the person in your building who coordinates volunteers or the teacher you notice using volunteers most effectively.

Volunteer Presentations

When you have a volunteer scheduled for a class presentation, communicate with him or her several days before to give specific information: the exact time the class meets, the number of students, what they are currently studying, how the volunteer's information will fit in, and tips on what will appeal to the students. Volunteers are usually taking time from their jobs to work with your classes, so it is unrealistic to expect them to meet all your classes for an entire day. Solutions to scheduling might be for the volunteer to meet a different class every few days, or to engage several volunteers to speak on the same topic during the same day.

Bear in mind that, even if your guest speaker is a former teacher, she or he will be apprehensive facing your class. (Remember your first day?) Do everything possible to prepare a successful experience. Explain to your students the day before what is going to happen and specify expected behavior even if the speech is Sahara Desert–dry. Provide a clean podium or speaking area along with requested supplies and equipment. Write the speaker's name clearly on the board and have coffee or water available. Try providing the refreshment in a school-logo cup and then make the cup a thank-you gift. Volunteers often leave your class exhausted, wondering how you get through a full day in one piece.

If you are unable to greet the speaker, send a student to meet and escort your guest. After the volunteer has been to your class, send a letter of thanks. Also send a letter to his or her supervisor acknowledging the employee's volunteer time and support of education.

Partners in Education

There are people and businesses in your community that are more than willing to participate in the education process. Some districts enjoy an organization called Partners in Education. Schools are linked with community businesses and, sometimes, with professors from the university in that city. Each partnership forms a committee of business people and teachers to decide how the business can serve the school and how the school can serve the business. For the most part, direct contributions of money are avoided. The business partners might provide:

- field trips, career guidance, career "shadowing"
- guest speakers
- large meeting space for PTO fund-raisers
- access to specialized electronic equipment and operators for special projects
- access for teachers to company training meetings
- tutors for accelerated math or computer students
- classroom helpers who come on a regularly scheduled basis
- judges for the school spelling bee or science fair
- organizers for a spring field day

In turn, the school might:

- stage musical performances during noon hours, meetings, and holidays
- provide coat-checking services for corporate meetings

- send student-made cards to all the employees involved in the Partners in Education project
- help decorate for a holiday, or work on the company float for a parade
- join an envelope-stuffing campaign
- participate with the business in a community service project
- compete on a business team at a community fun day
- provide complimentary tickets to sports events

The university affiliation might help the school by:

- contributing professional textbooks and research material
- providing tutors
- making appointments for students seeking admissions to the university
- providing specialized resources and experts
- providing individuals to help with special curriculum projects

The use of community resources can be as creative as the people planning the program. Small communities, for example, have embraced the Partners in Education concept but have modified the structure to include the whole business community and form a partnership with the town's one high school, one middle school, and one elementary. The committee only need ask, "Would it be possible . . . ?"

Other Volunteer Activities

Other volunteer activities or parent-generated activities in a school might include:

- arranging field trips to offices and manufacturing sites for career exploration
- collecting and delivering used books and magazines to supplement the library collection or to use for classroom enrichment projects

A Volunteer Listens

- producing a parent newsletter
- planning and supervising the all-night, nonalcoholic senior graduation party
- planning an all-school field day in the spring

STUDENT AIDES

In some schools, students who have a study hall period in their schedules choose to function as office or teacher aides. Depending on school policy, these students may or may not get a grade and credit for their work. Usually the individual teacher makes the choice whether to have a student aide or not. These students, depending on their skills, can provide a variety of services. They might create bulletin boards, file music or papers, wash desks, return books to the library, deliver messages, or type your study guides. They might be in charge of cleaning and storing equipment, textbooks, computer disks, or manipulatives.

Do not utilize student aides to type tests, discipline other students, or keep your grade book up to date. These tasks remain *your* responsibility. When training your aide, stress from the beginning that grades and other information she or he sees pertaining to your students is not to be shared with *anyone.* Insist on integrity and loyalty from your aide. If you do not get this loyalty, sign the student back into the study hall and complete those tasks on your own.

Your aide should not "cruise" the building and wave at friends through open classroom doors. If you do not have a specific job for your aide on a particular day, have him or her bring a book and read quietly or do homework for other classes.

CONCLUSION

Your day in school runs more efficiently with the help of a variety of ancillary personnel, both paid and volunteer. These people are part of the school program because of their strengths and support of the learning goals. These staff members and volunteers are worth getting to know, both as the providers of services that you are not in a position to offer your students and as potentially interesting friends. Make time to introduce yourself to these people and ask about their jobs and responsibilities. Ask about schedules and availability. Knowing about their job helps you best utilize their skills when planning a successful program for your students.

chapter ten

Families

I need to keep a log next year on all the phone calls I made to parents, all the parent meetings, and all the students I had to discipline.

Kent Rhodes

Many years ago Betty was sitting in the lounge with colleagues. Her principal walked in and asked what she was teaching in her fourth-period class. Because Betty had been thinking about her second-period seniors, her mind went blank. The principal said that a parent had called and accused Betty of teaching the occult. Betty laughed in dismay and nervous confusion and mustered an uneducated, "Huh? I don't even know anything about the occult." Betty's dear friend rescued her and told the principal that all the junior classes were currently studying the same author, with the objective of learning about writing that builds suspense through a series of small events tied to a surprise ending. The principal was satisfied.

It turned out that the student's stepfather had found a stack of books on the occult in his daughter's car. He was upset because many of them offended his religious convictions. The student had then explained that the books were being used to write a report for Betty's class. The parent called the principal.

This student had actually been working on a report that investigated haunted houses. Betty had approved this topic in relation to the author being studied in her class. After speaking with the principal, Betty immediately called to clarify the situation.

During the call, Betty explained the assignment. She acknowledged that she had approved the topic, but that she had done so without knowledge of the family's religious beliefs. Betty suggested that the report topic could have been one that was agreeable to all involved. She asked the parent to contact her directly if problems arose in the future.

CONFERENCES

Sometimes communication with families is most effectively handled by holding a direct meeting.

Conferences may be initiated by the teacher, the parent, or another staff member.

It's too bad that contact with parents often occurs after things go awry, but that's a fact of life. Parent conferences occur after a severe disciplinary infraction or after repeated attempts have been made to help the child academically. Even a meeting to plan a student's IEP (Individualized Education Program) can be a tense situation for parents or caregivers.

Many parents or caregivers have unhappy or embarrassing memories that cloud their perception of the entire education process. Many feel threatened when surrounded by educators. Many arrive angry because they had to take time from work, incurring the boss's anger.

Occasionally a parent will initiate a conference in order to give you information that will help provide a better learning situation for the child.

Managing the Conference

Any conferences about which you have misgivings should take place with a counselor or administrator in attendance. Before you call a conference, you need to have already established contact over the phone. In the case of a sudden disciplinary infraction, an administrator may make that contact. Conferences work best in a room where everyone can be seated informally around a table. Many teachers prefer having the student at the conference, but that is not always done. Allowing the student to attend the conference helps him or her accept responsibility for past and future behavior and also be a part of planning the course of action for change. A conference should not be punitive; it is a time to look for solutions.

When you walk into a conference, greet those you know and introduce yourself to those you do not know. Stand to introduce yourself if you are in the room before others arrive. Make sure that everyone has been introduced before the conference and that everyone has a chair.

When the conference is ready to begin, outline the issue. Check to make sure everyone understands and agrees on the matters to be discussed. Give everyone a chance for input into the discussion and the proposed solutions. Make a point of addressing individuals directly. Avoid using educational jargon. Talk about the potential you see in the student and your hopes for his or her success. Ask the student how he or she feels.

Do as much listening and watching during the conference as you can. You will gain insight into your student's behavior as you watch family interactions. Sometimes you will discover that a student's behavior simply reflects what is modeled at home. You will understand why a student picks on others or has a low self-concept when a mother calls her offspring "stupid" in front of teachers.

Marc remembers a conference that was called for behavioral and academic reasons. An administrator had called in several teachers to discuss the issues with the parent and the student. The parent offered an opening remark that effectively illustrated the root of the problem: "You're not going to tell me anything I don't already know—I know my kid is stupid." While the girl squirmed uncomfortably, head hanging, the administrator quickly stated, "The purpose of this conference is not to attack your family. We are here to find some solutions to help Tina be successful in school." Often caregivers will want to talk about personal school failures or problems rather than the child's situation. Sometimes you'll leave a conference marveling that the child is coping as well as he or she is in spite of the situation at home.

Parents may try to attribute the problem to anything else: the system, bad health, a divorce, another relative, or personality conflicts. You need to get the focus of the conference off placing blame and onto planning solutions that satisfy everyone.

If the parent or caregiver arrives angry and ready to scalp, draw on all your anger-management techniques: Listen attentively; restate what you hear; acknowledge the anger, but don't let it control the conference. If the caregiver's anger does not diminish, suggest that the conference be continued at a later time. If the conference does continue, you might ask the caregiver what specific things she or he wants to see happen: "What do you want me to do?" Then you can agree to the proposal, agree to parts of it, or state politely that you cannot agree to the solution because of (for example) curriculum restraints, school policy, or safety regulations.

Give everyone else at the conference an opportunity to relate their perspective and suggest solutions. Then, if the student is present, ask for his or her comments. Be sure the student agrees with the proposed solution. (The child often wants to cooperate and get back to class while the adult is the one being difficult.) Try to give the student as much dignity and control in the conference as possible. Afterwards, compliment your pupil on calm behavior and mention that it is not easy to sit in on a conference about yourself.

Unless it is a conference about grades, you don't need to bring your grade book or printout of you grades, but you will want to have your anecdotal record of the student's behavior and class performance. Do think about the student ahead of time, and rehearse a list of positive things to say, plan a short list of concerns, and think about possible solutions. Make it clear that you believe the student can be successful. At the end of the conference, thank everyone involved for his or her time.

Follow-up is necessary after a conference. A contract is one way to ensure understanding of expected behaviors and provide follow-up. Contracts can be written and signed by the student, family member, teacher, and administrator. A behavioral contract will include expected behaviors and consequences for noncompliance. An academic contract will set realistic goals, including a time frame for completing missing assignments and improving in-class participation. A realistic contract length is two weeks. At the end of two weeks, you will review the contract and determine if there has been improvement or if a stated consequence will occur. When the contract is signed, mention to the student that you feel good about the process and anticipate success. File a copy of the contract in your folder of student records. Make phone contact within two weeks, detailing student progress. Keep the student informed of progress as well.

Elementary Conferences

If you are an elementary school teacher, you will have regularly scheduled parent–teacher conferences in addition to those conferences called for special purposes. Elementary schools usually have conferences twice a year: in the fall after the first nine weeks, and in the spring after the third nine weeks. These conferences are held for teachers to share:

- student progress
- goals for the year
- areas of concern
- ideas for working with the student
- curriculum information

Mike remembers his first parent–teacher conferences as stressful events. He was nervous and overwhelmed at the prospect of having to schedule, prepare for, and meet with all fifty-two sets of kindergarten parents. You'll be nervous too, at least in your early years of teaching, as conference time rolls around. Don't dismay. Everyone else is nervous as well. Parents and caregivers are usually anxious about what you are going to say. If you aren't feeling a few butterflies, you may not be prepared. The majority of your meetings will be productive and go smoothly.

It is essential that you be prepared for conferences. If questions come up that you can't answer, make a note of them and find the answer later. Get back to family members in a timely manner by writing a note or calling.

Some teachers and students plan and hold these conferences together. The student prepares his or her portfolio and plans what he or she will report as progress, goals, and areas for improvement during the next grading period. The teacher and student spend time rehearsing for the conference so that the student feels confident and that all the information the teacher feels is necessary will be included. The student then runs the conference with input from the teacher and caregiver. Conferences of this nature provide an opportunity for students to demonstrate their competence, thereby gaining self-confidence and self-esteem.

PHONE CALLS

Rehearse phone calls in your mind or make some notes if necessary. When you call, clearly state your name, school, and connection with a specific child. Then pause to make sure you have the correct family member and that the person realizes who you are. Because many parents have remarried, last names and relationships have to be clearly established at the beginning of a call. Ask if you are calling at a convenient time. State the reason for your contact and give specific details. If the call is about discipline, use the "I am concerned and I need your support" approach. If the caregiver is not supportive, simply restate what has happened and what will happen if the inappropriate behavior does not stop. Thank that person for his or her time, and end the phone call. Document the conversation. Gary notes all calls made and keeps a list of dates in his grade book or anecdotal records. Later, if he needs to refer the student to an administrator, he'll indicate he has followed through with the discipline steps and can give dates of family contact.

It's best not to delay either relating successes or asking for help and support in solving problems. Return phone calls as soon as possible. If you return a call and find out a parent has left the office or is not at home, leave your name, a message that you returned the call, and a time when you will try again. It can be inappropriate not to return a phone call promptly when you've previously expressed concern about a student.

Since most parents work, it's best to try to make calls at a time when they may be reached at home. If you cannot contact a caregiver at home after repeated tries, leave a message at his or her place of business, listing specific times when you can be reached. Use discretion here. Some parents may not wish coworkers to be privy to their child's problems at school. Often a phone message with no explanation may trigger immediate assumptions of misbehavior and can precipitate unnecessary conflict between the parent and child. If you feel that a message may cause turmoil, it is best not to leave one. You must use good judgment in contacting families.

Mike looks for ways to make positive home contact. One winter, when an unexpected snowstorm closed schools two days early for vacation, he called each of his kindergartners to wish that child a happy holiday and leave assurances that the class celebration would be staged when the students returned. Mike was a hero to his students and their families.

REPORT CARDS

Messages to call parents right after report cards are issued usually do not foretell words of thanks. Look over that student's grades before you return the call. Recalculate the grade to double-check the math. Have the grade book or a printout with you when you call. Frequently a disappointing grade is a result of several missed assignments. Many students think if they forget several assignments, the bad news will simply go away. It doesn't. When you return the call, state the facts and comment on what the student can do to improve the grade. Mention the call to the student. Follow up with another phone call or note in several weeks.

ACKNOWLEDGING POSITIVE BEHAVIOR

After acknowledging a positive behavior in class you might inquire, "Would you like a call or note home?" Have the student write down a phone number, the caregiver's name, when you should call, and where you will be calling (home, office). Write the note or make the call that day if at all possible. "I'd like to share with you something very positive that happened in class today . . ." You might consider mentioning to a class that if ever a student needs a positive call home, you will be glad to make one. Barbara got such a request years ago when the driving age in her state was fourteen. The student wanted her to report good grades in order to obtain parental permission to take driver's education. Barbara told the student she would call and report the grades, but she would not endorse driving at fourteen. Barbara laughs and tells her students she will make positive calls but won't promote their private agendas.

PUBLICITY AND NEWSLETTERS

Publicity tells the public, families, administration, fellow teachers, and other students about successes. Every time you post a paper or project, you are publicizing student success.

If you have completed a project that involves student-choice awards, you might want to invite an administrator or a colleague with a free period into your room to view the projects and hand out the awards. Most get into the spirit of it and ham up the presentation, to the enjoyment of your students. One colleague stages an elaborate "Academy Awards" ceremony after her classes make their spring videos. Another holds an "Olympics Ceremony" celebrating students' accomplishment at mastering the multiplication facts. Families should always receive special invitations to such events.

Your school or your parent group might produce a newsletter that is sent to all families at intervals throughout the year. Make it a goal some time during the year to write a short article for this newsletter about an unusual project or one that enjoyed exceptional success. Include student names and a photo or two. Check your school's policy regarding release forms for students' photographs and work.

Another version of publicity might be the "Friday Folder." Each child in Kathy's elementary school purchases or is given a blue, two-pocket folder. During the week, all student papers go into that folder after marking. On Thursdays, each teacher goes through the folders, adding positive observations from the week, commenting on papers, and any other necessary communication to the parent. Students take these folders home on Friday, have caregivers look through the contents, sign the folders, and return them on Monday. Although this is time-consuming, the teachers in Kathy's school agreed that it is an effective method of communication with the home.

During an end-of-term review, Betty decided that her classes could produce a newspaper while studying for their semester exam. She divided her language arts classes into groups of three. The students brainstormed a list of all stories, skills, and concepts covered during the term, and each group chose one item from the list. After much discussion, each group prepared a short article reviewing that unit. The students shared the writing with other groups for additional information and editing help. Each article was then carefully rewritten. Students who loved using the computer pasted these articles into a newspaper format complete with the title each class chose for their "newspaper." She printed a copy of this newspaper for each student to study and made sure the semester test reflected those units the students emphasized in their projects. While reading their creations, students discovered a coupon on the back that entitled them to five points on the next test if papers were taken home, shared with parents, and returned with parents' signatures.

Some districts employ a person to do school-wide publicity in the community. If you are attempting to get television or radio coverage of a classroom project, this person would know whom you should contact first. Then, this publicity person would be at your big event to get pictures, names, and the story for district publication.

Robert videotapes his class performing readers' theater and class plays. The class members then take turns checking out the videos and taking them home to share class activities with families.

Whether you choose a formal or informal plan to tell families about what is happening in your classroom, the results will be positive. Students are pleased to have their successes made public, and parents become more supportive when they are kept apprised about classroom activities. Such an informed caregiver will also be a motivated homework tutor who is supportive of the entire school process.

ACCURACY IN CORRESPONDENCE

Any written notes, letters, reports, recommendations, e-mail, or other communication from you must be accurate. Check for spelling and grammar. A newspaper columnist in Marc's community received a letter from a teacher that was, unfortunately, filled with careless spelling and grammatical errors. That columnist had a heyday ridiculing the teacher in his newspaper. The embarrassment reflected on every other teacher in the community. Take the time to be accurate; your professional image is worth it.

If writing isn't your strong suit, scribble out a rough draft, then recopy it. It is appropriate to send notes home to parents in your handwriting, but first write a draft. You might ask a colleague to proofread the message to see if it says what you want it to say. Then recopy it onto a fresh sheet of school stationery.

Keep a dictionary on your desk along with a basic grammar book or a copy of *Writers INC.*, for quick reference sections on grammar, usage, and typically misspelled words. Those few minutes spent in correcting are worth the trouble and save you the embarrassment of sending out error-filled correspondence. Don't doubt for a minute that the general public will point out any written error they find in your writing. It is amazing how often, during a conversation, a parent will mention erroneous correspondence sent home by some other teacher or department. When corresponding with the family, try to avoid using current educational phrases. Most people won't ask for a definition, but they may feel inadequate for not knowing what you mean. They may feel as if you're talking down to them. This is analogous to your physician's or your mechanic's using technical terms that leave you baffled. Your message should be clear and to the point. If the document requires it, type. In this age of computers with spell check and printers that take school stationery, every teacher can produce error-free, professional communication. Learn how to use these resources. Letters home, recommendations for college applications, and material for publication must be sent error-free. Anything less diminishes your credibility. The appearance and construction of the typed letter or handwritten note are like a photograph of you and your teaching. Make sure your hair is combed and your shoes shined.

BACK-TO-SCHOOL NIGHT/OPEN HOUSE

No matter how many years you've been in the classroom, you're likely to have butterflies before open-house night. Some secondary schools hold open house one evening early in the fall so that caregivers may follow their child's schedule and visit each classroom for fifteen minutes. An all-school reception concludes the evening. Robert's elementary open house allows time for teachers to address families, followed by a time to look around the room and ask questions about curriculum and programs. These tips will help you get ready for open house:

1. Make sure your room is neat. Wash desktops and hang current student work on every bare wall. Have students help. Post your name and room number prominently outside your room and on your board. You could also post class lists by your door for parents to check to make sure they are in the right place. Dress professionally.
2. Type out an agenda for what you are going to talk about and, if applicable, include in it a copy of your class syllabus (see page 233).
3. If you teach middle, junior high, or high school, write the names of the classes you teach and a brief outline of the curriculum you cover during the year.
4. Display copies of the texts and support materials that will be used during the year.
5. Greet parents. It is amazing how many parents sit in or near their child's seat without knowing it.
6. Introduce yourself to the group and give a bit of background on the class. Explain your

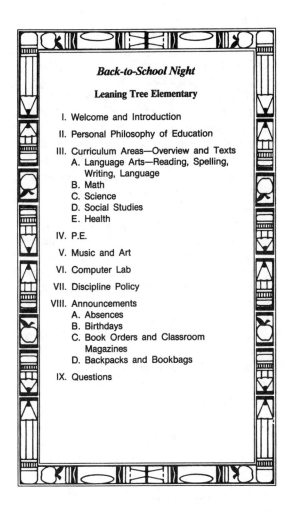

Back-to-School Night

Leaning Tree Elementary

I. Welcome and Introduction

II. Personal Philosophy of Education

III. Curriculum Areas—Overview and Texts
    A. Language Arts—Reading, Spelling, Writing, Language
    B. Math
    C. Science
    D. Social Studies
    E. Health

IV. P.E.

V. Music and Art

VI. Computer Lab

VII. Discipline Policy

VIII. Announcements
    A. Absences
    B. Birthdays
    C. Book Orders and Classroom Magazines
    D. Backpacks and Bookbags

IX. Questions

teaching philosophy and grading procedure in relation to the course curriculum. Talk about the text. Talk about your homework expectations.

7. Ask for questions.

8. *Do not* discuss individual grades that night because it is a get-acquainted time. If guardians inquire about grades, tell them you will call them the next day, or suggest a conference.

Betty, whose classes are studying Emerson's and Thoreau's essays during the week before the annual school open house, has her students do research on a country they'd love to visit. She next has them create a large picture postcard on 8" × 11" paper from that country to their parents. The message is to reflect the students' understanding of transcendentalism and how a person can experience another place without actually traveling there. These postcards are delivered to parents at the open house. Tami's open-house presentation includes a display of students' science lab projects in progress. Robert has his students direct their daily journal entries to their parents. He quickly glances at the writing that afternoon (he doesn't need a surprise on this of all evenings). Robert then invites family members to read and respond to their child's entry. He checks to make sure that all students' entries have comments at the end of the evening. He fills in the voids. Gerry's choir performs for the closing reception. Theater students can perform skits and pantomime. The idea is to provide families with a sample of what is occurring in the school.

PTO/PTA

Parent/teacher organizations and associations can be found at every level of public education. Their function is to support the educational process. This support might be in the form of volunteering, chaperoning, fund-raising, planning classroom parties, committee work, or workplace/school partnerships. You might be expected to attend a certain number of these meetings every year. It is a good opportunity to meet and get to know families, and you can gain some insight into their perceptions about what is happening in the classrooms. Attending these meetings shows your willingness to be involved in the total educational process and your interest in working with parents.

CONCLUSION

It is always important for you to keep the lines of communication open. Involve your students' families in the educational process as soon as possible in the school year. Be prompt in advising them of any difficulty or success. Look for creative ways to celebrate the good things that happen in your classroom. Make any communication specific and accurate. Take time to listen to parents' concerns as well. In all communication, verbal or written, be respectful and aware of the needs and emotions of your audience.

chapter eleven

Wellness

When your desk becomes buried and chaos has taken control, go home, rest and live to teach another day!

K. Merkley

Erin Grant

My advice for new teachers, is to find balance. Often, it seems as if new teachers choose all work, and no play, or just the opposite. They need to balance between very difficult & challenging assignments, and fun, energizing projects.

Melanie, a first-year teacher, arrived in Betty's room with a gray face, wide eyes, and an anguished look that said, "I'm desperate; I need to talk."

In a shaky voice, she proceeded to tell Betty that she was doing the best she could. In the course of the last two weeks she'd been fighting with her husband because she'd been up until 2:00 A.M. working on lesson plans, her evaluation from her principal had been disappointing, her toddler had been acting out at his child care center, and papers were multiplying faster than she could grade them. As the tears burst forth, Melanie looked at Betty through bleary eyes and said, "I left a job that paid me almost twice as much as what I'm earning now as a teacher. I don't need this."

If this sounds remotely familiar, this chapter is for you. You will find that taking a few deep breaths, reevaluating priorities, and making some effort to manage your stress will make life a bit easier. All people, at one time or another, feel frustrated and helpless for a variety of reasons. You are not alone.

Teaching certainly can be stressful, and your first years of teaching may be especially so. The stress will come from expected and unexpected sources. You will become a juggler balancing school and home life, professional demands, and personal needs. Unfortunately, when the "to do" list gets long, the first things to be dropped seem to be personal plans, time with family, exercise time, even sleep time. We urge you to think about making specific plans for your personal needs. It is too easy to neglect yourself. Yet, if you do, everyone suffers—your students, fellow faculty members, your family, and *you*. You must deal with how you feel about these situations and how you will deal with these many life stressors.

If you allow excessive, inappropriate stress to rule your life, you will find that you catch colds more easily, snap at a student who needs attention, miss a teachable moment, or miss the success of a hard-working student. You may forget to turn in required reports or purchase orders. A gentle reminder from your school secretary will sound like a reprimand.

Fun? No. Controllable? Yes! Keep thoughts about personal wellness at the forefront of your mind. There are always ways to cope with the job and keep your life in balance. Your physical and mental health is an essential factor in your teaching success.

CHOOSING PRIORITIES

Reasonable levels of stress keep you motivated and eager to teach. However, excess stress builds when you feel frustrated and out of control. Stress mounts when you have too many demands on your time. Setting priorities and sticking to them will help you stay in control. Answering the questions on the "Important-to-Me List" will help you set those priorities.

Important-to-Me List
- Are weekends exclusively for my family?
- What do my children need to do after school?
- How am I going to balance family, religion, school, and community obligations?
- What is more important, my teaching or my coaching?
- Is the overnight return of papers more or less important than detailed lesson plans?
- Am I going to follow the curriculum to the letter or teach curriculum based on other criteria?
- When or where will I fit in my personal time?
- What activities will help me relax?
- Do I have to keep the second job to make ends meet?
- How am I going to handle continuing my education?

- How will I demonstrate my competence to my administration, students, and parents?
- How do I regain control when I begin to feel stressed out?
- Do I know when to say NO?

STRESS MANAGEMENT

Years ago Allen was feeling particularly stressed out, and his doctor gave him some valuable advice. Allen was advised to make a list of everything that was bothering him. Allen was then to classify these complaints into three lists:

1. Those problems he could do something about.
2. Those problems that he had no control over.
3. Those problems that really didn't matter.

Then the doctor told Allen to rip up the second two lists and work on only the things he could change. It was a relief to Allen to throw away two-thirds of his worries!

You may also develop the habit of thinking about what is bothering you and ask, "Will this matter in five days? five years?" If the answer is no, then let it go and relax.

Betty carpooled for most of her professional career. Besides saving gas money, it was a great stress reducer. Betty's car pool provided sympathetic listeners who were willing to rehash the day's battles, trials, and victories. Those fellow riders shared experiences with Betty, and the level of empathy was high. Betty was able to arrive home with the difficulties of the day fading away. She walked in the front door more relaxed and ready to focus on the needs of herself and her family.

If you don't feel comfortable sharing your frustrations with fellow teachers, find another source of support. Stress can reach a level that becomes impossible to manage alone. Seek counseling. Some communities and area school districts have worked together to provide employee assistance programs where people can go for professional help. The consultations are confidential and support the theory that an individual whose personal problems are under control is more effective in the workplace. The fees associated with employee assistance programs are often covered by health insurance. Many teachers use these services.

Another place you may go to find support is the Internet. Your professional organization or subject area organizations have online Web pages that list discussion groups or chat-rooms. Exchanging ideas, frustrations, questions, and successes can often provide the needed outlet to help manage the daily stresses. If you are using the school computer and your e-mail address at work to access Internet information and support, be aware that your name and school will be "seen" at every site you visit. You don't need the added stress of defending your Internet usage and any non–school-related locations.

Knowing Your Limits

A major component of stress management is to know your limits. You need to be sensitive to the signals your mind and body send out when you are reaching the overload point. A large part of dealing with your stress includes forgiving yourself for what you can't control or can't get done. Use the following checklist to analyze your limits.

Adequate Sleep   How much sleep do you need every night? Occasional late nights won't hurt, but consistently losing several hours of sleep to work on plans or grade papers will not translate into better teaching. Begin to look for shortcuts and reevaluate your priorities. Your job demands an incredible amount of energy, and you often don't realize that fatigue is creating a hindering web around you until it is too late.

Prime Time   When do you do your best work? Betty almost never grades past 8:30 P.M.; if she does, she dreams about those essays all night. She tries not to grade on Sunday night because then she feels out of control and behind in her work. Determine when your most productive times are. If planning on Thursday after school makes your Fridays and weekends go smoothly, then try to accomplish it that way every week. Pay attention to what feels right and what doesn't. This simple change may eliminate some of the stress in your life.

Evaluations and Observations   You may feel anxious when dealing with administrators. Betty once confessed that she still feels extremely stressed out before every observation—even after so many years of teaching. Stress is a natural component of performance. It is only normal that you will want to impress your administrator during observations and evaluations. Share with your administrator what is happening in your classroom and solicit advice when you need it. Your administrator may become your ally and partner in creating a strong learning environment.

Saying No The word is *no*. N-O. No. Practice saying it because you can't attend every meeting, bake for every bake sale, or drive the car pool to every soccer game. Especially during your first years of teaching, give yourself the gift of time. Choose projects that are personally satisfying for you. To the rest of the requests reply, "I really appreciate your thinking of me, but I don't think I'll be able to participate at this time."

Students will also ask you to sponsor, chaperone, or participate in their class activities. You will feel complimented, but do not agree without thought. Find out how much time you will be expected to commit and what you will be expected to do. If what students are asking you to participate in makes you feel uncomfortable (being a candidate in the "Kiss the Pig" contest for example) decline politely. Kindly reply, "I have an allergy to pigs, but I'll be glad to sell tickets." If you have already been assigned to sponsor a club or coach a sport, you probably do not need to add any more responsibilities to your day.

Returning Assignments Don't promise a specific date for returning assignments. Tell students how many papers you've already graded and how many you have left to evaluate. Set daily goals for yourself for how many papers you will grade. Share with your students how much time you spend grading and preparing. It helps them get a sense of your job as well as appreciate that you are working hard in their behalf. Try to balance grading the daily work and the larger project assignments. Betty set the goal to always have papers returned within two weeks. There are some assignments that she grades very carefully, while other assignments get a completion grade. A completion grade is a notation in the grading program that the work has been completed and turned in on time.

Doing Your Best   You must not allow school to dominate your every waking moment. If it does, you will burn out. You can't teach every item in the curriculum, reach every student, or make everyone happy, so don't feel frustrated when it doesn't happen. Decide what you can teach in the allotted time and do your best to accomplish this. How many times have you told your students, "Just give it your best"? They expect the same from you.

Outside Class   Carefully consider the time you have outside the classroom. Taking an evening class your first year of teaching may overburden you. On the other hand, being part of a class for first-year teachers may provide a support group. A recreation class might release tension.

Coaching and Club Sponsorship   Coaching and being a club sponsor may be knitted into the fabric of your teaching responsibility, especially in the early years. It is a fact that many new teachers are assigned duties, clubs, and coaching assignments beyond basic teaching responsibilities. If your assignment includes coaching, overseeing the school yearbook, or newspaper, be sensitive to the extra work and stress that it will add. Try to cosponsor a club with an experienced teacher so you won't have to invent the shortcuts for managing club activities. Seek a member of the faculty who has previously worked with that group as your mentor. If you are assigned to a club that deals with money, introduce yourself to the person in charge of your school's business affairs and make an appointment to learn about the procedure for collecting money and making bank deposits.

Time Out   When you feel yourself losing the battle, catching a cold, or getting angry too easily, take a break. Don't do any schoolwork for an evening or a weekend. Go away if necessary. Soak in a bubble bath. Take a long walk or run. Go to a movie or dinner. Cook a fancy meal. Go to bed with a good novel. Have some chocolate. Pamper yourself.

Moving On   If you feel as if you have lost, forgive yourself. Think about the limit you went beyond, and decide what you have to do to avoid that pitfall next time. Get on with your life.

Feelings of Insecurity and Challenges   Insecurity causes stress. You may be highly versed in your subject area or have received rave notices from your student teaching supervisor. You may even have years of successful work history under your belt. There are still many situations that leave teachers—novice and veteran—feeling out of control. Insecurity can breed stress, fatigue, and health problems if it is not dealt with appropriately.

Student Challenges   No matter how many education classes you've attended, degrees you've hung on your wall, or how well you've planned your lesson, students will challenge the whole process. "Why do I have to learn this?" "We didn't do it this way in Ms. D's class." "I didn't want you for my teacher, but my mom said I had to be in here." "This is stupid." "This is boring." "That's not the way you spell it." "This isn't fair."

The last comment is absolutely correct: It isn't fair—to you. Yet some students have always perceived that their duty in life is to challenge authority. They do it to novice and veteran teachers alike. So take a little comfort in the fact that we all get those challenges every year. Don't take such comments personally. Students challenge authority and power rather than you personally. Don't react overtly, get flustered, or enter into a verbal debate with the student. The more you plan to involve students and allow them to make connections between the learning and their personal worlds, the more they will be engaged in learning and less likely to challenge.

Challenges from Parents Unfortunately, students are not the only ones who will question your procedures and motives. Parental comments can be equally hurtful. "I was really hoping that Bobby would get Mr. _____ for his teacher." "Are you sure that this is the best way to teach my child? Her teacher last year never asked her to do it that way." "What does my child have to do to get an A?" "We are going to be out of town next Friday. Pat won't miss anything, will she?" These questions can come from concern for the offspring more than a desire to personally attack you. When talking to these parents, you might share with them the unit plans you are working on or give them ways to reinforce learning. "Please ask Brie to tell you about the poem she coauthored with her group today. It is really a lovely piece." Make parents your allies and partners from the beginning of the year by keeping them informed about their child's successes and needs. Make a point of sharing what is happening in your class through student-authored newsletters, phone contacts, brief conversations after school, or at parent meetings.

Grading Challenges Humans are not the only sources of stress. Grades often cause tense moments. Students frequently question grades on tests, essays, or report cards. They may approach you and inquire in a strident tone: "My mother wants to know how come I got a B when I aced the semester tests." Many teachers may give in because a nagging student simply wears them down. Model a lesson on manners. Students who make inquiries in a respectful way are listened to and receive your attention. However, students have even been known to discuss which teachers are easy marks for such manipulative behavior. You can lessen the blow of such confrontations.

1. Before you hand back a test or essay, announce that you will not engage in a grade-debate during class. Tell students that you will gladly discuss the grades if they will make an appointment with you. Ask them to bring along the test or project they would like to discuss. Students with legitimate concerns will do this.

2. Return papers at the end of the class period, unless you are going to focus on them during that day's lesson. You don't want them to spend time paging through the graded assignment or stewing angrily rather than focusing on the lesson. If you are going to use class time to reteach some concepts, then it is appropriate to hand back papers at the beginning of the class.

3. You are not infallible. We all write poor test questions or make grading errors. There is nothing wrong with eliminating a test question if you notice that the majority of the students misunderstood what you were asking. You can also change a student's grade if he or she points out an error you made when adding up the total. Letting the student know you did not intend to make the error and changing it sets the tone that we all make mistakes and we simply fix what we can and go on with things.

As you deal with students, parents, and administrators on a daily basis, your personal feelings occasionally get assaulted. You may feel rage, frustration, envy, and despair. You will feel alone, isolated, and helpless. You have to consciously let those feelings go. You must focus on what really matters: teaching to the best of your ability and taking care of yourself.

Pacing

Thoughtful pacing of lessons can make a difference in your personal wellness. Some days you will be energetic, have tons of activities, and know exactly what must be done by Friday. The lesson plans will call for frequent change in activities: You present some new information, help students to take notes, move students into groups, have students return to report back to class, and take a short quiz—all in the course of one block of time. The pace of the class will be quick, energetic, and often noisy as students work on maps, short stories, posters, research, or skits.

Other days you will want your students to proceed through the lesson thoughtfully. A slower pace doesn't mean that your lesson is underprepared or that the students will be out of control with nothing to do. Rather, it means that you have planned activities that engage students independently or in small groups. This slower pace might include project choices that appeal to different learning preferences: drawing, reading, writing. This slower pace allows you to monitor individual progress by walking around the room or holding conferences with individual students.

Alternating the pace of your day or classes will help eliminate some of the stress you may be feeling in your life and provide variety for students. On the days you have all the energy in the world, keep the activity level high. When you are feeling overwhelmed, know that you can plan slower-paced lessons where students will still be engaged in learning. The trick is to find the balance for yourself and your students.

Getting Along with Others

Becoming entangled in uncomfortable situations with other staff members is another way to add stress to your life. No matter how well chosen, every faculty is going to have its differences, rivalries, and jealousies. Teachers who survive these complications without getting involved usually display a high degree of self-confidence and a ready sense of humor while staying objective. You will quickly recognize the gossips, the complainers, and the troublemakers. You can be friendly with these people, but beware of forming close alliances.

Be careful whom you talk to and what you say. You might make a comment about a staff member, assuming that it will not be repeated just because your listener is your next-door neighbor. It would be uncomfortable to discover that your neighbor reported directly back to that staff member. Especially during your first year at any school, practice patience. Stay out of "office politics," and keep your barbed comments to yourself. Figure out what the administration expects of the faculty and work toward that goal. If you are supportive of your administration and colleagues, they will likely be supportive of you in return. This support can do wonders for your self-confidence and go a long way toward ensuring your personal wellness and job satisfaction. If you find yourself in a conflict with your administrators, begin looking for a job elsewhere, but do not become insubordinate while completing your present assignment.

Seek out positive friends. They will motivate you and share ideas. Listen to these wise colleagues. Surround yourself with people who make you feel good about yourself. These people will be happy to see you and interested in your success. When you feel positive about your teaching, you will be happy and will discover that you are growing professionally and developing a variety of interests.

Finding Your Mentors

If you are a beginning teacher, or an experienced teacher starting at a new school, you will often feel lonely, isolated, and overwhelmed. This is normal! Ideally, your building or district will have a mentoring network that will meet with you and other new teachers periodically. If you find yourself in a situation where no mentor is assigned, lis-

ten and watch carefully in order to identify someone in your building who you think could become
your mentor.

In your first weeks and months of teaching
you will discover supportive colleagues. You may
identify with kindred spirits and form relationships with people willing to share your tears, frustrations, failures, and successes. It may take
longer to find friends who will listen compassion-
ately, respond supportively, and keep your secrets
confidential. People will not be willing to enter
into a trusting relationship if you complain or continually degrade your present teaching situation.
Cherish the people who give you support and return the loyalty. You'll find that you will soon be a
mentor yourself.

Being Absent and Being There

It is a fact that if you are a normal human being,
you will catch your share of colds and flu bugs.
This is especially true for new teachers exposed to
so many new germs. Your first defense is to be
sure that all your immunizations are up to date—
for your sake as well as your students'. You can't
wash your hands enough. This is sound advice but
not always possible with schedules and distances
to the restroom. You will get sick. The debate is
then whether to "tough it out" or stay home. Being
in school often spreads your germs to the kids, and
then you have to wrestle with make-up work. If
you go to work sick, you will take longer to get
well and often catch the next germ more quickly. If
you are sick, stay home.

Often teachers and students come to school
too sick to be productive or they self-treat for an
ailment when they ought to be at home or in a doctor's office. Teachers also find it difficult to get
doctor's appointments after school hours, so the
stress of waiting only adds to the frustration of not
feeling well.

There are times when it seems virtually impossible to be absent: A field trip, a guest speaker,

or an assembly is scheduled that you are responsible for. Your obligation is to notify other adults
involved. Let them know that you are sick and that
there will be a substitute taking your place. Ask
the school secretary in charge of checking in substitutes to notify him or her of a note you've faxed
in or that you need to speak on the phone. Have
the phone number of the substitute contact person
and the fax number of your school at home. It's
also a good idea to take these numbers with you
when you go out of town, in case you find yourself
stranded.

If you are suddenly sick, you need to get
help. Press your call button, summon your neighbor, send a student, phone the office, or let some-
body know you need help. If you must leave the
room, be sure a neighboring teacher knows you
are out of the classroom. If you let students know
that you are not feeling well, they will usually be
concerned and will be open to an alternate assignment that will not require your active participation. This will allow you to survive until a
substitute can be located or you make it to the
end of the day. As hard as it is to believe, things
can go on without you.

SUBSTITUTES

Planning for a Sub

It may seem like more work to plan for a substitute than it is worth. Using a substitute will be
easier if you follow the plan for preparing a sub
folder as outlined in Chapter 4.

Be sure you have a sub folder prepared with
emergency lesson plans and that this folder is at
school. Then stay home. This is the time when that
rainy afternoon you spent writing emergency
lessons you thought you'd never use will pay off. If
you have a chance to write lessons before you go
home sick, plan a single lesson or short unit, covering several topics that will enrich what the students are currently studying. Structure the work

so that the sub has to collect, evaluate, or grade what the students do. Everyone has to be held accountable for completion of the lesson. Include a note to the sub that lets him or her know you need information about how the class progressed.

Depending on your school district's policy concerning extra textbooks, you may want to have a copy of student texts or teachers' manuals at home. This can be a lifesaver when you are sick and at home for a few days. You can alter plans or talk with your substitute via phone or e-mail about where to find materials.

It is helpful if you know by the end of the school day whether you will need a substitute for the following day. This is helpful for the person who calls substitutes, and you might get your choice of who will temporally replace you. Plan *extra* work for each class period or subject area with clear instructions. Few subs can fill in extra time effectively. It is better to provide detailed plans for them. Advise your neighbor of your pending absence and ask that he or she check on your sub during the day.

Sometimes you or a family member will become ill during the night and it will be necessary to call a sub early the next morning. If your lesson plans and seating charts are easily located, you may simply notify the appropriate person and go back to sleep. Sometimes you will need to get additional instructions to your substitute. Your spouse or a family member may have to deliver plans to the school office. If you have a close friend at school, a phone call to that person communicating lesson plans will solve your problem. You might ask that your sub call you if he or she has any questions after reading your lesson plans.

Returning after a Sub

Learning to cooperate with substitute teachers and coping with unexpected change are realistic social skills for students to develop. Occasionally the diverse personality that covers for you may be a "real weirdo," according to your students. Talk to your class about dealing maturely with substitutes.

If you return to a room full of problems, have a discussion about behavior and responsibility. Make it clear all year that you expect your classes to be courteous and cooperative when you have a substitute, student teacher, intern, or guest in your room. If a substitute administers a justified punishment, hold students accountable for their behavior. A phone call to parents will reinforce the point that the students' learning must proceed whether you are in the classroom or not.

One spring Barbara was absent for two weeks, recovering from surgery. Although Barbara left detailed lesson plans, the students did not accomplish what Barbara had expected. Several students had done their best to sabotage the plans and the substitute. Barbara returned to pandemonium. Students all wanted to tell their side of the story. Barbara assigned a journal entry identifying what the students learned, what problems they encountered, and what they would do differently the next time they had a sub. She couldn't avoid the surgery and had prepared for the sub. Beyond that, Barbara couldn't feel guilty about what happened; and neither should you in similar situations.

Sub Survival Kit

One year Tami, a fourth grade teacher, and her partner went out of town on a long-awaited ski vacation over the President's Day holiday. It was just the break Tami needed during the busy second semester of her first year teaching. Tami planned on getting home late Monday afternoon and spending time preparing for class Tuesday. When she and her partner rose early Monday morning to load the car for the trip home, they discovered the car had been stolen. This changed Tami's strategy of having time to plan before returning to school Tuesday. Because Monday was spent filing police reports and making alternate travel plans she also had to miss a day of school. If things weren't stressful enough, Tami had to spend time and money on the phone finding out whom she needed to contact to get a sub.

This incident convinced Tami that she needed to have essential information handy for emergencies. Now she has a list of needed fax and phone numbers that she takes with her when she is going out of town.

Emergency numbers to have:

- Substitute call-in number.
- Preferred sub's number. (If you want a specific sub, call this number first. Then notify the sub call-in service so they won't waste time calling this person for another assignment.)
- A colleague's home phone. (This person could help the sub find needed materials or the sub folder.)
- Your principal's home number.
- The school's phone number, so you can notify the office when you will return or if you need to retain the substitute for another day.
- Your school's fax number in case you need to send additional plans or instructions.

FATIGUE

Occasionally you won't feel cold-in-the-head sick, but you will experience an overwhelming sense of fatigue. Teaching demands huge amounts of energy, and even emotional fatigue can leave you feeling as if you have been filled with more lead pellets than "The Celebrated Jumping Frog of Calaveras County." Identify what energizes you and make time for it! Ellen attends a yoga class once a week. Brian takes walks every lunch hour. Barbara quilts. Mark makes time for a daily run and would never miss his daily vitamin supplements. Exercise helps. Fly a kite with the neighborhood kids. Walk to the post office instead of driving. Go down to the river with your kids and feed the ducks. Sit on the porch and watch the sunset. Spend time working in your garden. Go to bed early. These simple actions can help you avoid illness and the consequent absence from school.

RENEWAL

One way to ensure personal wellness is to plan times of renewal. The fatigue-relieving strategies mentioned above are minishots of rejuvenation. These might be weekends you spend on short excursions with family or friends. Even if you feel in control of your teaching situation, you will be surprised how much more energy and focus you will have if you allow yourself time for recharging.

Joining an interest group outside the school community can provide a refreshing perspective. Seek groups simply to have fun with people you enjoy. These associations can contribute to your positive self-image as a whole person, not just as a teacher.

School breaks offer time for personal renewal. Many teachers take jobs during off time to make financial ends meet. A non–education-related job could be refreshing. If you still want to work with young people, camps or organizations of every focus would appreciate your expertise. Working for the National Park Service might provide a welcome option. There are many additional types of seasonal job opportunities.

Renewal could also come in the form of volunteering. Your local Assistance League or hospital auxiliaries can always use a helping hand.

Some teachers peruse grant applications the way others read seed catalogues. Grants and fellowships will pay for you to attend universities and colleagues around the world or close to home. Lists of these special programs can be found in professional journals, on the Internet, or in information from sponsoring organizations. Many of these programs are designed to increase your content knowledge and assist you in designing effective lessons. Others may attract you because they focus on a topic you have never had time to study before. Your district may encourage you to attend a specific seminar, conference, or class to prepare you for a new teaching assignment.

Travel is another tempting option. Teachers are eligible for reduced rates on trips planned especially for educators. Other teachers facilitate groups of adults or students, often earning free or reduced passage for them. Information about these programs can be found on the Internet, in professional journals, and from teachers' associations.

Whether you decide to spend your breaks working, volunteering, traveling, or attending classes, view the break as a time to relax and focus. You will find yourself looking forward to the next challenge—still nervous, perhaps, if you are a new teacher or you started the year in a new situation, but a lot more energized and self-confident.

CONCLUSION

Personal wellness is not given enough consideration. Make time for yourself, your family, and your friends. Find ways to get away from the daily concerns of teaching. Take care of your mental and physical health. When you are sick, stay home. If you plan ahead, you can be away from school without undue stress.

Accept that you cannot be the perfect teacher and reach every student—no one can be that perfect. If there is something that you didn't teach or handle to your satisfaction, make a note of it and handle it differently next time. Forgive yourself. This will go a long way toward improving your personal well-being.

12

Dispelling
the Myths

When you feel like you have done nothing right,
take time to look back on your successes.
Take time to listen and then ask a lot of questions.
develop your own style. You will see lots of wonderful
teachers but remember to be yourself.

Rosie Stoldt

If you're like most people, you left college in a glow of idealism. With your head packed full of teaching theory and educational jargon, you may have entered the profession with these ideas:

All students will like you. (After all, you're nice to them.)

Students will always be enthusiastic about you and what you teach.

You can be your students' pal.

There is no such word as failure.

Master teachers are born that way.

Let's examine these teaching myths.

MYTH #1:
ALL STUDENTS
WILL LIKE YOU

For a variety of reasons, this won't happen. It's likely that no matter what you do, you'll be viewed by some students as a villain. During these volatile times in students' lives, you may be perceived as the mother or father that the student, temporarily, can't stand. For some adolescents or children, anyone who represents authority, in any capacity, is suspect. If Jamie and her boyfriend have had a fight minutes before entering your class, you and what you have to say will be as significant as a mosquito. Recognize and accept that you will not be a hit with everyone every day.

MYTH #2:
STUDENTS WILL ALWAYS BE
ENTHUSIASTIC ABOUT YOU
AND WHAT YOU TEACH

Depending on the grade level, the time of day, the season, and the weather, the enthusiasm of students is as predictable as a hurricane.

The day after Halloween or the day before vacation often guarantees that students will be giddy
with enthusiasm. Homecoming games and athletic
events spark similar excitement. Sometimes this
vitality carries over into the classroom and en-
hances the classroom experience; sometimes it has
the opposite effect and kids are too wound up to
stay on task. Careful curriculum management suggests that you plan high-interest activities that can
channel the enthusiasm positively.

For most new teachers, the realization that
kids aren't enthused each day and that some never
appear to be is devastating. Don't believe that all
students will be motivated all the time. Too many
factors prevent this, such as home problems,
health problems, and social problems.

MYTH #3: YOU CAN BE YOUR STUDENTS' PAL

Betty's father, a master teacher and educator for
thirty-three years (though he's retired, he's still a
master teacher), used to tell Betty that, ultimately,
she was in control. She could establish any type of
classroom atmosphere she wanted. He also told
her that subject competency would never be a
problem and that classroom management would
present the greatest challenge. He was right.

If any piece of advice in this book deserves the
most emphasis, it's this: Do not be your students'
buddy. Through your voice, dress, and expectations,
remember that you are the teacher and adult role
model. You want your students to respect and respond to you, not think of you as one of their peers.

MYTH #4: THERE IS NO SUCH WORD AS FAILURE

You've been reading about tips for success. Many
are formulas to help plan lessons, to deal posi-

tively with human beings, and to succeed as an educator. If only teaching were so easy!

What no one may have told you is that, unlike the salesperson, teachers don't always reap instant rewards. The test may measure the grasp of the information studied, but the smile or nod may be merely a student's political tactic. Most teachers don't know the actual effect they've had on their students.

If daily lives ran according to formulas, students would express and feel regret when they had cheated, insulted, or lied. Ideally, the formulas would result in a classroom where all the students appreciated you being there and felt that learning was a privilege. These same students would be on time, always be present, and take pride in their work. Most teachers leave the university with heads full of knowledge, assumptions, formulas, and, fortunately, an agenda for success. However, as difficult as it is to accept, failures will occur, and nothing you can do will change this.

Because most teachers wish for success for their students, failures can be devastating. An explosive comment from an angry student, a failed test, or a withdrawal from class or school can disappoint you. Do not take these as personal failures. It's okay to feel let down, but if you've made students aware of consequences and expectations, you are not responsible if they choose not to comply. Don't enable students. If they have made choices to fail, do not feel that you have failed.

Lessons will flop no matter how well planned. It happens to all teachers every year. Analyze what happened and structure the next lesson to avoid these pitfalls.

MYTH #5: MASTER TEACHERS ARE BORN THAT WAY

A colleague of Robert's was once overheard to say to a beginning teacher, "I'm a master teacher because I was born that way." This statement might be humorous if it weren't such a falsehood. To be a master at anything takes years of trial and error, experimentation, and the ability to learn from past mistakes. Whether it be in classroom management or curriculum planning, master teachers continually encounter new students, material, and situations. Master teachers are not born as perfectly formed educators. They do not allow themselves to stagnate; they continually grow and improve.

THE TRUTH ABOUT TEACHING

Teaching is one of the most demanding and challenging of professions. After reading this book, you may even wonder about your career choice. We'd like to leave you with some final thoughts about why, in spite of its challenges and demands, teaching is rewarding enough to attract millions.

Unlike the business world, there is no "bottom line" in teaching. You often don't know the impact your sales pitch has had on your clients, at least not immediately. What does make an impression is an occasional letter or note from a student that says, "You taught me so much." "Your French class gave me the tools to study and gain this job that I love." "I never liked to read until I took your class." "The other students in my math class at college were lost, but thanks to you, I know this stuff." "You were the best teacher I ever had!"

Sometimes you'll hear about your successes in a most unconventional way. An acquaintance of Barbara's had been seated on a plane next to a former student of Barbara's. During the 800-mile flight the young lady revealed to Barbara's friend that if it hadn't been for Barbara, she would never have written well enough to give herself the confidence to apply for the position she held. The impact of a teacher may last a lifetime. Rarely can other professions make the same statement.

Teachers have a great deal of autonomy. What happens in the classroom is largely up to the instructor. While others in the work world complain about having so little control—deadlines, phone calls, and sales calls—you, for the most part, plan your day.

You have an opportunity to see human beings at their best. The enthusiasm and honesty of kids is a treat to witness. While adults often have their beliefs carved in stone, young people are still developing their own values. Your role as a model has a major impact on this.

Teaching offers an opportunity for continuous growth and enlightenment. Each new prep, collegial chat, or article provides new information. You continually learn as you teach. Nowhere except in the field of education are you daily in the company of so many experts on subjects ranging from science to Spanish. You have a wealth of knowledge at your fingertips because of the environment you work in.

If teachers feel frustrated about salaries and benefits, there is comfort in knowing that time is money. The time teachers have for renewal and growth is precious. The teaching profession allows opportunities for travel and continued education. Few careers offer a period for such renewal and growth, providing a chance for a clean slate each school term.

The responsibilities of a teacher are mind-boggling. As you embark or continue on your journey, we'd like to leave you with a thought: The effective teacher trains students to surpass his or her own capabilities. May you, like Mentor, influence those who follow.

Professional Associations

American Alliance for Health, Physical Education,
    Recreation and Dance
1900 Association Drive
Reston, VA 22091-9989
www.aahperd.org

American Association of Physics Teachers (AAPT)
5112 Berwyn Road
College Park, MD 20740
www.aapt.org

American Association of Teachers of French
57 East Armory Avenue
Champaign, IL 61820

American Classical League
Miami University
Oxford, OH 45056

American Council on the Teaching of Foreign Languages
    (ACTFL)
6 Executive Place
Yonkers, NY 10701-6801
(914) 963-8830

American Counseling Association
5999 Stevenson Avenue
Alexandria, VA 22304-3300
www.counseling.org

American Federation of Teachers
319 N. Front Street
Harrisburg, PA 17101-1203
(717) 236-7486
www.aft.org

American Home Economics Association
1555 King Street
Alexandria, VA 22314

Association for Educational Communications
    and Technology
1025 Vermont Avenue, NW, Suite 820
Washington, DC 20005
www.aect.org

Association for Supervision and Curriculum Development
1250 N. Pitt Street
Alexandria, VA 22314-1453
www.ascd.org

Council for Exceptional Children
1920 Association Drive
Reston, VA 22091-1589

Council for Learning Disabilities
P.O. Box 40303
Overland Park, KS 66204

International Reading Association
800 Barksdale Road
Newark, DE 19714-8139
www.reading.org

International Society for Technology in Education (ISTE)
1787 Agate Street
Eugene, OR 97403-1923
(503) 346-4414

Music Educators National Conference (MENC)
1902 Association Drive
Reston, VA 22091

Music Teachers National Association
The Carew Tower
441 Vine Street, Suite 505
Cincinnati, OH 45202-2814
www.mtna.org

National Art Education Association (NAEA)
1916 Association Drive
Reston, VA 22091-1590
www.naea.org

National Association of Biology Teachers (NABT)
11250 Roger Bacon Drive
Reston, VA 22090

National Business Education Association
1914 Association Drive
Reston, VA 22091-1596

National Council for the Social Studies
3501 Newark Street
Washington, DC 20016

National Council of Teachers of English
1111 Kenyon Road
Urbana, IL 20016
www.ncte.org

National Council of Teachers of Mathematics (NCTM)
1906 Association Drive
Reston, VA 22091
www.nctm.org

National Education Association
1201 16th Street, NW
Washington, DC 20036
www.nea.org

National K–12 Foreign Language Resource Center
Iowa State University
Ames, Iowa 50010
www.educ.iastate.edu/currinst/sflrc.html

National Middle School Association
2600 Corporate Exchange Drive, #370
Columbus, OH 43231
www.nmsa.org

National Science Teachers Association
1840 Wilson Boulevard
Arlington, VA 22201-3000
(703) 243-7100
www.nsta.org

index